# Education Can
# *ONLY* Be Offered

# Education Can *ONLY* Be Offered

## How K-12 Schools Will Save Democracy

Don Berg

ISBN: 0999488805
ISBN 13: 9780999488805

# Contents

# Introduction

How would you respond to this job offer? It was posted by a dad after his daughter received it.[1] The job has

- her do work that is useless to others and is routinely thrown away;
- no job description: she just has to do what she's told;
- no salary and no equity (she'll get experiences that are presumed to be valuable);
- a boss that she is assigned to each year who cannot fire her (and she will not be allowed to quit due to a long-standing government edict);
- required micromanagement by her boss—project status is closely monitored, and she will be regularly ordered to change what she is working on throughout the day;
- work team assignments that are issued by bureaucratic tradition based solely on her birthday; her previous experiences, vocational goals, and cultural background will be consistently ignored;
- no access to a reasonably neutral system of conflict resolution; her boss and her boss's boss within the same building are, typically, the

only resources for conflict resolution (no unions are available to her, though one or both of her bosses may be unionized); and

- no opportunity to participate in a democratic system for altering the decision-making processes that created and maintain the organization.

His daughter rejected it. In consultation with her father she opted out, even though millions of other seven-year-olds accepted identical offers to do school work. With only trivial adjustments, the same offer is being extended by nearly all public, private, and charter schools. In fact every state government has a law that attempts to impose this work on all young citizens. Why do we believe that children can learn how to live in a democratic society when they spend so much of their early formative years in such undemocratic organizations? Why do we believe that imposing work on young citizens can be educationally valuable when we know that imposing work on older citizens (a.k.a. slavery) is not only unhelpful but also both morally wrong and universally illegal?

But some children are living within democracies during their K–12 years. I know because I have taught in a school that is organized democratically and have studied schools like it both formally and informally for many years.[2] Unfortunately, they are a vanishingly small proportion of K–12 schools in most of the world so far. That means you are probably not familiar with them, and when I describe them, you are not likely to understand them. Let me put this in perspective for you.

Imagine that you and your whole family are in Independence, Missouri, in 1848, and you are about to set out on the Oregon Trail, a 2,200-mile journey. You are preparing to spend four months walking, with all your worldly possessions in an ox-drawn wagon. Every time you stop, you have to unhitch the oxen, tend to them, and provide for all the other animals you have along. It means constant wagon maintenance, foraging for firewood and clean water, cooking over open fires, and setting up and breaking down camp every day. There are no support services and no infrastructure along the way. You are risking the lives of your entire family. Disease, hostile people, wild animals, bad timing, and ill preparedness are all potential killers. Your odds of dying are one in ten. Even so, hundreds of thousands of people chose to take that risk in the 1800s.

Now imagine that back in Independence in 1848, I materialize in front of you and offer you the following proposition. I say that I have access to a flying machine called an airplane. I claim that it can take your family all the way to Oregon in one day instead of four months. The airplane will also reduce your odds of dying to less than one in one thousand, two orders of magnitude less risk. But the problem is, I don't know when in the next four months the airplane is going to be available to take you to Oregon.

The question is this: Which risk do you take? You are on the horns of a dilemma. Do you choose the familiar wagon mode of travel? Or do you choose the mysterious airplane mode, which some guy claims is much safer but is unfamiliar and operates on an unpredictable schedule?

The relevance of this imaginary situation is that I am going to tell you about democratic schooling, an educational opportunity for your family that is likely to be just as strange to you now as an airplane would have been to pioneers on the Oregon Trail in 1848. What we know about the long-term outcomes is that they are roughly comparable to mainstream K–12 schools. The basic outcomes such as being able to read, write, and do arithmetic will occur—but at an unknown time. We just can't predict when.

Regardless of the mode of transportation, those who survive the journey end up in basically the same place. The limited research on these schools suggests that they have an advantage, not necessarily in the outcomes but on the journey itself.

Democratic schools are a subset of holistic schools that, as a psychologist, I believe do a superior job of supporting kids on their *journey* to adulthood. But these kinds of alternative schooling options are unfamiliar to most people. They provide the basics, but the timing is unpredictable. The limited evidence available suggests they will reliably nurture your children. Regular schools are a known quantity, but they come with substantial risks and have a history of failing to nurture the children in their care.

You might wonder whether nurturing is properly the responsibility of a school. Aren't parents the nurturers while educators are just instructors? This misconception is based on a misunderstanding of how learning works. If learning were just the delivery of knowledge, skills, and information into the heads of the children, then it would be reasonable to expect that nurturing might be separable from schooling. It also might be reasonable to assume that making those deliveries is more important than honoring a child's desire to be in control of his or her own activities. Learning, however, is not that simple, and that desire is a lot more than a mere whim.

Learning can be shallow, fake, or deep. If you merely deliver, then the most likely outcomes are shallow and fake learning. Shallow and fake learning were probably fine in our preindustrial past, but in today's global society, it is no longer adequate for success, according to an impressive variety of leading authors and policy makers, such as the National Association of State Boards of Education, Sir Ken Robinson (a globally recognized expert on creativity in education), the Canadian Education Association, Yong Zhao (a respected scholar of international education), the Hewlett Foundation (a large-scale funder of educational innovation), and many others.[3] In order to get the kind of deep learning that is now required, there are psychological preconditions that must be in place in order to support deep learning. I use the term "nurturing" as a shorthand to refer to those preconditions.

There are three major symptoms of the systematic lack of nurturing in mainstream schools. The three symptoms reflect problems with how they fail to support the primary human psychological needs of autonomy, competence, and relatedness, which are three out of eight of the most basic components of nurturing.[4] Two symptoms that everyone knows about are: dropouts and underachievers. A third major symptom that everyone understands but few openly acknowledge is fauxcheiving—lacking mastery of a given subject despite attaining "achievements" for it in school.

Dropouts are alienated from school instead of welcomed into it. So they disengage from the school. Their psychological need for relatedness has been thwarted. According to a report issued by the National Center for Education Statistics (NCES) in 2016, the dropout risk was overall about one in seventeen, with the lowest risk for white kids at about one in twenty-two and the highest for Hispanic kids at about one in eleven.[5]

Underachievers experience schools as a controlling place where they do not have adequate self-expression. So they disengage from the majority of classroom activities. Their psychological need for autonomy has been thwarted. According to the 2009 High School Transcript Study, also from the NCES, one in four graduates are below curriculum standards.[6]

Fauxchievers experience schools as an arbitrary system to be gamed. So while they might seem engaged in school generally, they are emotionally disengaged from some or all of their subjects and do an absolute minimum of work to get whatever level of scores or grades they deem necessary. Their psychological need for competence has been thwarted. According to Howard Gardner at Harvard University, who is famous in education circles as the originator of multiple intelligences theory, at least half of those who go on to advanced degrees in their field do so by fauxchievement.[7] This means they are unable to solve the most basic problems in their field when those problems are presented in a real-world manner rather than how they would have been presented on a school test.

So, no matter how you slice it, there is a significant risk that the school system will cheat your child out of some or all of the education they deserve. In fact, the odds are worse than what the pioneers on the Oregon Trail faced. Your child can be cheated in several ways, but the odds of being cheated are good if you stick to typical mainstream schools, regardless of whether the school they attend is public, private, or charter.

In mainstream classroom schooling today, if we ask, "Who has which powers in this organization?" the answer will amount to the same command-and-control "industrial" education system that was cobbled together under the pressures of unprecedented population growth and urbanization in the 1800s, using the hottest new organizational models of the day.[8] In rough outline, the system is based on a hierarchical distribution of power in which an elite few at the top of the bureaucracy are given effectively dictatorial[9] decision-making authority. Those who are subjected to the arbitrary decisions of the higher-ups are not provided with meaningful recourse if they find the decisions objectionable; this is true of both teachers and students.

The governance structures that monitor and modify the behavior of schools are not designed to elicit, let alone take seriously, the thoughts and ideas of students and only rarely that of teachers.[10] Schools in the United

States are, ironically, thoroughly undemocratic. Despite a century or more of sound criticism of that undemocratic character and a few weak attempts at reform (e.g., student councils and certain legalistic or bureaucratic appeals processes), the power structure remains fundamentally unchanged for most children and their teachers. This situation strikes me as odd given not only our national aspiration to being a democratic country but also our claim of being the very origin and inspiration for all the other democracies in the world.

Homeschooling parents have taken on this challenge personally. They may not think of themselves in these terms, but they have flattened the power structure completely. By becoming DIY educators, they are giving their children the experience of having direct access to the decision makers. You can't get much more democratic than that. I am not going to address homeschooling as a movement in this book, but I encourage homeschoolers to read on because most of the points I make about the schools I studied apply to that movement too. One of the schools I studied formally was a homeschool resource center which showed the same positive characteristics as the democratic school in the same study.[11]

The schools that have taken the lead on implementing real democracy have, not surprisingly, come to call themselves "democratic."[12] They use the term as a framing to encompass a wide variety of practices that are all intended to enable young people to have access to real power to affect the course of their education. The movement has never come to consensus on a particular definition of the term, but they do share a consensus on how important it is for children to have the ability to make decisions about their education. They accomplish that task in so many different ways that every proposed meaning for the term seems to leave out one or another school, model, or philosophy. They were formerly known as free schools in the '60s and '70s, meaning "free" as in freedom.

For almost ten years, I have had a set of Google alerts constantly bringing to my attention stories on the Internet that mention "democratic schools" or the names of specific ones. My impression is that it is a rare event when there is a fair representation in the media that articulates how democratic schooling produces educational value. Any coverage is rare, but coverage that goes in depth to explain the high quality of learning that is possible is even rarer.

Due to the radical differences in the power structure between them and the mainstream schools, they only rarely get access to public funds, and so the vast majority today are private schools charging parents a tuition fee that is usually on the low end of the scale. They are often portrayed as places bordering on wildness, with children and adults freely roaming about doing seemingly random activities. Even if the community members are observed doing something that might be labeled "educational," they are likely to be doing it in a manner that is normally regarded as recreational.

In the typical mainstream classroom, there is an adult teacher who is given the power to boss children around without the children having the ability to object to the bossiness. The bossing part of the relationship between adults and children in mainstream schools is generally regarded as the very archetype of classroom activities. If you ask a group of four-year-olds to act out school, they will inevitably figure out who gets to be the teacher, and then that person gets to be bossy. The "teacher" will try to be nice, but if they do not get enough obedience, then they will arbitrarily punish their "students" (who will quit the game if the bossiness gets too egregious, an option not available to students in real schools). And when mainstream students do something that would normally be considered "recreational," they may be required to do it in a manner that makes it seem more "educational." In other words, the teachers will impose requirements that they deem to be important without having to justify their decisions. No one will question the authority of the teacher, even if the additional requirements kill the fun and recreational value of the activity.

In the mind of the average person today, the hierarchical organization of the classroom probably seems like an ideal teaching environment, whereas a democratic school community might appear to be a strange arrangement for children. To the uninitiated, democratic education may appear to lack the necessary leadership of adult authorities. These images and the usual judgments that result are very ironic and might be funny, if the personal and moral stakes weren't so high. The judgment demonstrates a fundamental confusion about what education is and how schooling can serve to bring it about.

In this book I shall compare mainstream and democratic styles of schooling to give you a clear view of this confusion. While both forms of schooling can be functional strategies for the perpetuation of society, the moral obligation of parents and neighbors to nurture each individual child suggests that more democratic schooling options are generally preferable and various forms of democratic power should become central features of mainstream schooling in the future. Despite my narrative choice to enhance the apparent contrast between these ideals of schooling, in the real world there are schools all across a continuum that exists between them. This book is really just me lamenting the fact that the democratic side of that spectrum is still so unknown and underappreciated.

The first chapter, "Schools Are a Reproductive Organ," takes the perspective that schools are a system for complex literate societies to replicate themselves across generations. Drawing on the logic of biological procreation among a population of individual organisms (i.e., frogs and humans), I suggest that among a population of societies there is an equivalent continuum of trade-offs to be made. Each society makes some form of trade-off between investing in the highest quantity versus highest quality of information in the replication process. There is no question that all the strategies in the continuum have proven successful at the reproductive function, but it is time to consider the consequences of the trade-off more clearly and explicitly.

The second chapter, "The Illusion," takes a deeper look at the illusion that education can result from adults imposing academic activities on children's lives.

In the third chapter, "Stewardship of a Child's Mind," I examine how the moral obligations of parents and neighbors toward an individual child interact with their moral obligations to perpetuate society.

In the fourth chapter, "Dispelling the Illusion," I examine how we can move forward toward a preferred future by breaking the spell of the illusions that most people seem to have about education and by teaching democratic principles through the institution of schools. Using an analogy to our transportation system, I derive design principles and present a model of organizational participation so that we can learn from the holistic schools that are leading the way.

# One

## Are the Mainstream Strategic Trade-Offs Worth the Cost?

The strategies of organisms that reproduce sexually are easily placed on a continuum between the two extremes of <u>low-energy</u> investment in each individual but with a *high rate of generating new individuals* (e.g., plants and insects) versus <u>high-energy</u> investment in each individual but with a *low rate of generating new individuals* (e.g., birds and mammals). They are both objectively successful strategies for biological reproduction since both forms have withstood millions of years of sustained existence.

Frogs, for example, are closer to the extreme of producing prodigious quantity. I am very familiar with this fact because just outside my bedroom window is a lush frog habitat. In the spring the frog chorus gets so loud that it can drown out our Netflix. The frogs invest their reproductive resources in the production of a high number of fertilized eggs, but ultimately the parents abandon their offspring to their individual fates. As a reproductive strategy, the gamble is reasonably successful because so many eggs are laid that even if just a very small percentage succeed, the species continues to survive.

The extreme other end of the spectrum is human reproduction. We have not only reduced the number of individuals produced but we have also extended our investments of energy beyond merely producing another physical individual. We are required to nurture each individual for well over a decade to ensure that our cultural and social information are reproduced along with our genetics.

Let's look at two key variables in the biological reproduction continuum. First there is some general ratio of adults to fertilized eggs. Over the lifetime of a female individual, there are repeated cycles of fertility. A mama frog is fertile for six years of her ten-year life-span.[13] Conservatively, if she lays about 4,000 eggs once every year, then in her lifetime she will bring into the world over 20,000 offspring. Some female frogs may produce as many as 200,000 eggs per year so there may be potential for over a million offspring from some froggy matrons. Compare that to human women who are known to have given birth to anywhere from zero to sixty-nine children. Since about 1800 most women have given birth to less than seven, with the majority of women in developed countries today averaging less than three. To simplify the ratios for comparison, we are looking at roughly the difference between 1:7 (or less) in humans and 1:20,000 (or more) in frogs. The crucial point is that there is at least a difference of four orders of magnitude, reflecting utterly different strategic investments. Both ends of the spectrum are successful from the species standpoint; the nature of the difference reflects fundamentally different strategies that vary in another way.

The second key to the variance is a quality that characterizes the ways that the energy for reproduction is invested. In the frogs-versus-humans example, we can see the difference in the relationship of the parents to the offspring after they have been brought into the world. The frogs abandon their progeny, so their investment in nurturing is extremely low; humans bond with their children and use about a quarter to a third of each child's expected life-span to plow even more resources into nurturing them.

| Individual Reproductive Trade-offs | High Volume of Offspring | Low Volume of Offspring |
|---|---|---|
| High Nurture | *Too costly to be viable* | Humans |
| Low Nurture | Frogs | *Too ineffective to be viable* |

Given that schools serve the reproductive function of a society, the continuum of reproductive strategies is based on transferring various symbol-manipulation (academic) skills to young people. What are the options for transferring the necessary symbol-manipulation skills? The two basic extremes on the continuum are as follows:

**The Froggish Strategy:** Investing in frequent repetitious participation in symbol-manipulation activities in the context of weak social structures, which default to coercion, to get young people to participate in these activities in the hope that some of the symbol-manipulation skills will be transferred.

**The Human Strategy:** Investing in the generation of a strong social structure in which every child who participates is generously nurtured to become capable of recognizing the necessity of acquiring the symbol-manipulation skills available to them and then having support available to help them follow up on that insight.

Given the domination of industrial classroom schooling in education today, our society is currently favoring the froggish strategy. The mainstream industrial classroom schooling process discards or otherwise neglects many individuals. If the system is ultimately just about the survival of society, it is successful. Using that strategy means that individual children and teachers are merely expendable fodder for the societal reproduction process in the same way that individual frog eggs and polliwogs are expendable fodder for the reproduction of their species. It is inherent in the design of the hierarchical industrial power system in mainstream schools that a great mass of sacrificial individuals are necessary to produce the few that will carry the society forward.[14]

Democratic schools are an example of holistic education in which the students are seen as needing more than just academics to be well educated. There are many models of holistic education, and I suspect my main points apply to most of them too even if they don't self-identify as democratic.

| Societal Reproductive Trade-offs | High Volume of Academic Activities | Low Volume of Academic Activities |
|---|---|---|
| Strong Social Structure (Holistic) High Nurture | *Too costly to be viable* | Democratic Schools |
| Weak Social Structure (Coercive) Low Nurture | Industrial Hierarchical Schools | *Too ineffective to be viable* |

These extremes of strategy suggest that there is roughly an inverse relationship between the strength of the social structure and the number of discrete academic activities that each child will participate in before enough mastery of the skills will be established in the population. This formulation may sound odd if you expect coercion to be labeled as "strong" and other forms of social structure to be "weak."

As a motivation psychologist, I consider the strength of a social structure to drive the level of engagement of the individuals who are conforming to the dictates of that structure. Engagement means that the individual is proactive about participation and contributes to the process. More engagement means the structure is stronger; less engagement means the structure is weaker. From the perspective of self-determination theory,[15] which is one of the most widely supported theories of human motivation, coercion usually indicates a weak social structure. It tends to diminish engagement rather than enhance it. The quality of motivation that follows from coercion is low, and the learning produced by low motivation tends to be shallow. So the trade-off that is inherently made in mainstream schooling is to have generally weak social structures (tending toward coercion) that are used as the means of motivating children to participate in as many academic activities as they can manage to cram into their days.

Maximizing the number of academic activities is simply a necessary consequence of the weakness of the social structures used to induce compliance. We can assume that some degree of academic symbol manipulation is required to function in our global society today. Coercing participation in academic symbol-manipulation activities causes the learning of those skills to be shallower rather than deeper. As I mentioned before, an impressive variety of experts and leaders have also pointed out that our complex globalized society is not well served by shallow learning.[16] Therefore, in order to get the degree of skill required to reproduce our complex globalized society, mainstream schooling must raise the number of activities each student will participate in due to the poor quality of learning that follows from the coercive tendencies of the system.

Democratic schools, on the other hand, invest in nurturing all of their students to be socially capable individuals. Democratic schools raise the quality of motivation so that the number of academic activities that must be participated in does not have to be so high. The better motivation means that the quality of learning is superior. This enables the adults to relieve themselves of the burden of programming everything that a child does every day. In democratic schools (in most countries with advanced economies), the staff knows that the children are already embedded in a rich environment in which opportunities for academic symbol manipulation are abundantly available regardless of what the school provides. Since the children have an inherent biological program that drives them to become capable members of their human communities, they will sooner or later engage with academic symbol manipulation in order to achieve one or more of their goals. Even though they may not engage with academic symbol manipulation as often as in mainstream schools, they will learn those skills more thoroughly due to the high quality of motivation and engagement that the democratic environment supports them to bring into situations of academic learning. They succeed at reproducing society because the investment ultimately pays off with an extremely high proportion of productive, engaged citizens who learn deeply. The movement toward democratizing schools is growing, though it is still only a marginal segment in the overall field of education.

As mentioned in the introduction, the typical image of the democratic school as a wild environment implies that adults are not providing authoritative leadership; sometimes reporters hint at the possibility that there is a systematic undermining of societal expectations about how children should be "properly educated." For instance, when Dan Rather visited Sudbury Valley School in Framingham, Massachusetts, in 2001 for *60 Minutes*, he was openly incredulous that the children would learn anything of value. In 2007, John Stossel from Fox was also incredulous about Sudbury, and their story started with the usual implications that adults don't have a clue and that kids must be doing outrageous things. To her credit, Kennedy, the Fox reporter whom Stossel sent to Sudbury, did a reasonable job of addressing Stossel's questions. Democratic schools give implicit credence to some of the negative assumptions by marketing themselves as bastions of unbridled freedom. That framing, I suspect, may fail to communicate how the foundations of our democratic society are being effectively and efficiently conveyed through the constraints on actual behavior within the community's social structures. What the "freedom" marketing message of democratic schooling fails to convey is that the children are, in fact, actively constrained from doing harm or otherwise misbehaving. What the schools offer is not unbridled freedom, it is freedom constrained by a caring community organized to give children real power instead of having it actively denied to them by a hierarchical bureaucracy. Democratic schools make children act out democracy, not just sit through abstract lessons about how democracy should be enacted. The school structures include some combination of a mutual obligation to respect all members of the community, legitimate opportunities to participate in making the day-to-day rules (real governance), and mandatory participation in the structures that enforce the rules (at least when they are accused of breaking them).

Mainstream industrial classroom schooling, on the other hand, spends tremendous amounts of resources to ensure that the children entrusted to their care are a captive audience to be bombarded with an unceasing stream of symbols to be manipulated according to nonnegotiable dictates from higher levels of the system. Except for basic safety (most of the time), there is no sense that the system has any meaningful obligation to individual students other than providing the bombardment and encouraging the manipulations that they make the children endure. This was especially true under the federal legislation originally known as No Child Left Behind (an *extremely* ironic title).

The current power structure of the mainstream system ensures that our society will reproduce, but at the expense of many individuals. Gallup reports show that 70 percent of American teachers and 50 percent of students are disengaged.[17] Their estimation of the rate of student disengagement may be low. Other experts have estimated the rate to be closer to that of their teachers.[18] Shallow and fake learning are both overwhelmingly normal and expected in mainstream schools.

Both extremes of the societal reproductive strategy continuum have proven to be successful. Industrial schooling has been in successful operation since the nineteenth century, and democratic schooling has been in successful operation since at least the early twentieth century. I take the establishment of Marietta Johnson's School of Organic Education in 1907 in Fairhope, Alabama, as my reference point. They self-identify as a democratic school and were featured as one of a number of promising models of innovation in the 1915 book *Schools of Tomorrow* by John Dewey. There may be earlier examples that I am not aware of, but Fairhope Organic School is still in operation, so it's indisputable as a working model. Further, while the amount of evidence is severely limited, none of it has ever shown that anyone was worse off for having attended such a school.[19] Industrial schooling is the dominant mode of operation for schools worldwide. Despite that advantageous market position, there is growing interest in moving away from the froggish end of the continuum, and there is a strong and growing movement to democratize schools.[20]

# TWO

## Maximizing the Imposition of Symbol-Manipulation Activities Educates Children

In order to understand the pervasive illusion about education, we have to step back from the present. We have to step back far enough to get a wider perspective than that afforded by the illusion itself to see how it fits into a larger pattern.

The dominant illusion about education may have been formulated from the perspective of a peculiar view of human history that is no longer well regarded. In early history the primary sources of authoritative information were religious texts that used unsubstantiated rumors and ambiguous metaphors passed down from our oral traditions to describe what went on before. Unfortunately that view was severely limited. Western traditions, until relatively recently, have assumed that everything worth knowing about humans occurred within the past six thousand years. The extreme version even went so far as to promote the idea that everything in existence is less than six thousand years old.

But since then we have developed more precise ways of determining and describing what would have been going on in the deep past. I bring your attention to the following milestones:

16

## Decade Scale

Computer technologies                                        ~50 years ago

## Century Scale

Precomputer media (radio, telegraph, etc.)        ~100 years ago

Science                                                              ~500 years ago

## Millennia Scale

Mathematics                                                      ~3,000 years ago

Reading and writing                                          ~6,000 years ago

Agriculture                                                        ~12,000 years ago

## Tens to Hundreds of Millennia Scale

Spoken language or storytelling                      ~50,000 years ago

## Thousands of Millennia Scale

Origin of life (Optimizing states of mind)  ~4,000,000,000 years ago

The milestones go backward from our most recent innovation in symbol manipulation, the computer, and notes the rough time scale of each major advance in the complexity of our abilities. Most importantly I ask you to notice three things:

*First*, that the history of all the various forms of written and electronic symbol manipulations extend back only about six thousand years, which coincides with the transition from oral to written history and some inherited views of how long everything has been in existence.

*Second*, notice that agriculture and spoken language both predate reading and writing, the most widespread methods of storing and retrieving symbols in our current environments. With the development of agriculture, in particular, our species developed whole new ways of organizing how we control our own and other people's behavior for the common good.

*Third*, note that the vast foundation upon which all forms of symbol manipulation are built is our ability to achieve optimal states of mind.

What, you should be wondering, is an optimal state of mind? In short, achieving an optimal state of mind is the method that all living organisms use to survive. As the legacy of all our living ancestors extending back about four billion years, achieving and maintaining optimal states of mind is the ability to strike an appropriate balance between our internal states and those of the external world.

Organisms have the ability to detect some features of their external environment. That ability to sense the environment is necessary because organisms must maintain themselves through interactions with that environment. When an organism detects conditions that are going to kill it, then it has to do something about that situation in order to survive. Since it usually cannot change the conditions in the environment directly, it has to move into a different environment or undertake some form of transformation that is more suitable to survival. Individual plants don't move themselves, but they undertake reproduction in ways that can ensure the survival of the species at the expense of individuals who happen to end up in hostile circumstances.

You might wonder, since the first cells did not have brains like ours to house their mind, where was it? In some ways of thinking, my assertion here is nonsensical because minds are inherently associated with brains. But I prefer to use Dr. Dan Siegal's definition of mind[21] as the embodied and relational process that monitors and modifies flows of energy and information in an organism. Based on this definition, minds are not confined to brains. All cells are inherently concerned with these kinds of activities, so minds are inherent to all of life, not just charismatic megafauna like us. Minds are a fundamental part of being alive; brains are an add-on. In the catalog of features that life chooses from as it reproduces itself, a brain is a sexy option for high-performance minding.

The most fundamental task of living is creating and maintaining a balance between our internal states and the external world such that our mind is optimized, and, as a consequence, we maximize Life itself. Both individually and as a species, our life is a small part of the much greater whole of Life. If we, individually, fail at our task (as many before us have), then Life is diminished in some minute way. If we succeed (as all of our direct ancestors did), then Life is enhanced. This is true for all life. So far the enhancements have outweighed the diminishments, but there is no guarantee that the pattern will last forever.

A unicellular mind is severely limited, yet it still manages to react to its environment in a myriad of important ways that mere objects cannot. A plant mind has a variety of capabilities that enable it to transform the world and itself throughout its life-span. Think of how much of an effect a tree can have on a sidewalk when it grows close enough to push the sidewalk around and break it into pieces. When a tree grows up next to a fence, it can engulf the structure. Both man-made objects and the trees that interact with them can be transformed. Animal minds are even more sophisticated due to the necessity of moving around among dangerous enemies and challenging rivals. Some animals evolved brains to enhance the ability to keep track of threats and opportunities and respond more appropriately. Instead of using only their genes to embody the lessons they learn, they acquire and store lessons in their brains, too.

We humans, with our very special abilities to imaginatively simulate deep pasts and distant futures, have the opportunity to take this balancing act (between our internal states and the external world) to new heights. The balancing act enables us to make use of both our ability to attend to important things that are happening right now in this moment (similar to other life forms) and our abilities to look into the past and future to get an accurate sense of what can and should happen in subsequent moments (unlike other life forms). If we lose our balance in this particular challenge, then we can get completely absorbed in the now moment with all the infinite details of the universe or we can get lost in an unreal fantasy about the world as we wish it could be or could have been. In any of these cases, we may fail to anticipate either an imminent threat or a better opportunity; losing out in just the wrong moment could ultimately cause us to miss our chance to make a contribution to life, humanity, or just our family. Besides maintaining this balance, which optimizes states of mind, we have further enhanced our ability to learn by storing our lessons not only in our genes and brains but also in the artifacts of our cultures, first in storytelling and then in ever more elaborate and complicated forms of technological artifices that we use to embody our stories in the world around us (like this book).

You are familiar with the archetypical example of an optimal state of mind if you have experienced flow, the state of focused effortlessness that is described by high performers in every field when they are able to lose themselves (in a good way) in an activity. The more mundane versions of optimal states are usually described in neutral to positive terms like being focused, happy, satisfied, and so on (while nonoptimal states are described in negative terms like anger, confusion, depression, etc.). All of our emotions are potentially optimal depending on the situation, so it is not simply a matter of experiencing certain emotions. In his book, *Flow*, psychologist Mihaly Csikzentmihalyi (pronounced Me-high Chick-sent-me-high) says it is the ideal match of the challenge of a situation with our abilities to handle the situation. Thus, it is also a moving target. As our skills and abilities increase, the level of challenge necessary to achieve the flow of optimal states of mind also increases.

Consider that the illusion that misguides schools is based on the view that symbol manipulation is the most basic activity to be accomplished in education. In fact, achieving an optimal state of mind is an even more fundamental skill. Why do we manipulate symbols? We do not manipulate symbols for their own sake. We manipulate symbols to achieve something even more basic, optimal states of mind. This is a drive that we share with every living thing that has ever existed. Our apparently unique talent as a species to create and manipulate symbols can be a more elegant, refined, and complex technique for accomplishing that same basic function. The wisdom of over four billion years of life makes seeking optimal states of mind our most elementary—our most primary drive. As humans, we have opportunities to do this one thing in a huge variety of ways, often involving symbol manipulation.

Now consider a rough history of the power structures by which we control our own and other people's behavior for the common good. This is how we, as social animals, engage with others to achieve the results we want in the world. In the pre-symbol-manipulation era of life, there was one obvious rule for power structures that is still evident today: might makes right, and the strong and bold get their way. Of course, it's not really that simple, but it's a good rule of thumb. Once again there is a trade-off continuum between the following extremes:

The physically strongest and boldest get their way; thus you invest developmental resources in physical size and strength plus mental characteristics of aggression and decisiveness.

versus

The most socially connected with communicative influence get their way; thus you invest developmental resources in mental skills of emotional intelligence, cleverness, and ingenuity in conjunction with social skills that can lead to having access to the existing movers and shakers in the community.

The development of symbol-manipulation techniques makes the second option much more sophisticated than could ever be achieved before. In evolutionary terms, humans have made a commitment to the second strategy, which is evident when we are compared to our evolutionary cousins—gorillas, chimpanzees, and orangutans. Our long ancestry was committed to the first strategy long before the second developed, so we still have evolutionary programs that have us favor the strong and bold even within our sophisticated social networks. But, because of our ancestors' commitment to venturing across the continuum, we have a much greater range of responses than ever before.

The key thing to think about in terms of the different power structures is the efficiency by which each kind of power is maintained. The strong-and-bold method requires a person who is strong and bold to be present in order to manage his power. The social-connection-and-communication method can enable a leader to delegate the maintenance tasks to symbols that essentially reside inside a person's mind (and can be reinforced by cultural artifacts). The leaders who communicate effectively set up symbol patterns that remotely (via identity) do the work that strength and boldness are required to do in person.

The social power structures in human society today are based on establishing group identities that spell out standard sets of roles that are played by individuals. Those roles become automatic cognitive frames through which each person views their situation. A CEO of a Fortune 500 company knows what to do, how to dress, and what her responsibilities are to others. And, back when she was a second-grade student in school, all the answers were different, but she had equal confidence that she knew the role she was expected to play (even if she didn't *want* to play it). And the majority of the time it works without a hitch. Being complex living beings, we can sometimes be creative about how we choose to play out our roles, but we also have checks and balances in the system that ensure that the common good is ultimately served most of the time.

The education illusion essentially arises from our inherited myopic view of human history and what it means to be human. In previous eras we had the conceit to believe that we were created separate from and, more importantly, placed in a superior position above all other creatures on the earth. We thought we were supposed to be the strong and bold, getting our way among the species. We acted as if we had the powers of a god to determine our own and other species' (and people's) fates, independent of the consequences. We took our symbol-manipulation skills to be the very fundaments of our society and built schools that reflected all of these conceits. This view of humanity and its place in the world is wrong.

We exist on an ever-evolving creative continuum with all life that has been and continues to be developing throughout the course of over four billion years. We share the same fundamental drive as all other living creatures to optimize our states of mind. We just happened to have taken a path that enables us to reflect on this history and appreciate the blessings that God (or Goddess, or Allah, or whatever name you prefer for the ultimate cause of everything) has bestowed upon us. We are beholden to all life on the earth for the quality of our lives. While we have attained previously unimaginable powers, we are still dependent on other people and other creatures for our existence, and we would do well to remember that. As a species we will ultimately reap the consequences of our actions in spite of all our newly developed powers.

Now that we have a better understanding of our proper place as one of many species living interdependently on planet Earth, we can see that the illusion was not an intentional act against our own interests; it was simply an honest mistake based on our misconceptions about the world and our place in it. When we came to realize how powerful our symbol-manipulation skills were at changing our world, we gave it all due respect from the perspective we had at the time. Our view at the time was that our sacred books held our greatest wisdom and the indubitable secrets to the universe; therefore learning to manipulate the symbols to learn from and create books was crucial to our success. When we examined our history, it was evident that powerful authorities (parents, tribal or political leaders, etc.) played an important role in our lives; then, once again, we did our best to give them all due respect from the perspective we had at the time. Those efforts to honor the roles of symbol manipulation and authority led to the undemocratic schools that dominate education around the world today. Those schools long predated our current scientific understanding of learning as occurring at shallow, fake, and deep levels.

It is our mistaken assumptions about the primacy of symbol manipulation and the importance of obedience to, and imposition of, authority that cause false impressions about the educative value of the day-to-day behavior of students in democratic schools. From those same assumptions, the traditional classroom falsely appears to be a universally beneficial educational environment where teachers are authorized and encouraged to be the strong and bold managers of children's behavior for a significant proportion of their childhood years.

This view hides some key characteristics of the mainstream classroom. For instance, the power structure distracts children from attending to their natural processes of optimizing their own states of mind. When a teacher repeatedly interrupts a young child who is in a state of focused concentration just because the clock says an arbitrary period of time has passed, as determined by some distant authority as the appropriate amount of time for a child of that age to spend on that kind of task, then that teacher is communicating to that child that his or her being in an optimal state of mind is not important.

The tendency of schoolteachers to provide a constant barrage of symbol-manipulation activities becomes a barrier to efficient and effective acquisition of those skills. The barrier to deeper learning arises because the children are prevented from developing reliable access to optimal states of mind. They are too often hampered or interrupted in their efforts as they struggle with the nonoptimal states they encounter in the classroom.

What is hidden by our assumptions in the case of democratic schools is how they prepare young minds for their eventual instruction in symbol manipulation. That preparation makes the instruction so efficient and effective that it may not be in evidence on an everyday basis. So, in essence, the images of the different types of schooling show us the trade-offs in action. The typical classroom invests its resources in direct behavioral control by adults. That environment emphasizes imposing as many symbol-manipulation activities on children's lives as they can manage. Democratic schools invest their resources in a strong social structure in which children are empowered to discover the necessity of symbol manipulation to achieve their own goals and then support them to acquire those skills efficiently and effectively in the context of their community. This trade-off is explored in more detail in the next chapter.

# Three

## Parents and Neighbors Just Want Good Kids

When we realize that the foundation of deep learning is achieving optimal states of mind rather than the acquisition of symbol-manipulation skills, then we are forced to make adjustments to the basic terms we use to talk about schooling. We have to change our thinking to accommodate these shifts in meaning as we plan for educating our children.

Remember that optimal states of mind are the primary strategy that we have inherited from life itself to survive and thrive. Optimal states of mind consist of an ideal match between the state of the external environment and our internal states. They occur when we are able to conceive of an array of options for action that both (a) match actual options that are available and (b) provide us with some means for achieving our goals. When we are able to achieve optimal states of mind, then we not only survive but also we transcend the moment by thriving, ideally in a manner that enables others to thrive as well.

To start with, learning is automatic, unconscious, and impossible to avoid; it is as basic a biological function as metabolizing food. Everyone is learning all the time; the important question is this: What are we learning from the combination of power structures and exchange processes into which we have embedded ourselves and our children? The question of whether or not some set of symbols were manipulated in the right way is trivial in comparison.

Teaching is properly about the alignment of the context (the learning community's power structures and exchange processes) to attain mastery of whatever skills are necessary for accessing optimal states of mind. Teaching is about activating the growth of mental maps, enabling students to create ever more accurate representations of how the world works and how they can work effectively within it. Instruction, which is primarily about the delivery of knowledge, skills, and information, should be considered distinct from teaching because it is embedded in a different level of expertise. Teaching properly deals with shaping the context, whereas instruction deals with skillful application of particular behaviors within contexts (often with emphasis on the correct manipulation of symbols).

An educated person is one who perceives accurately, thinks clearly, and acts effectively on self-selected goals and aspirations, as they develop robust, dynamic cognitive maps of how they uniquely access optimal states of mind. (Notice that this definition of education, which is the intended ultimate outcome of schooling, strictly requires neither schools nor symbol manipulation.)

Schooling is about the creation of learning communities in which a dynamic variety of contexts are made available to students such that they can apply and further develop their skills for achieving optimal states of mind in each context. (Notice that in this way of thinking, families can be counted as a form of schooling.) Ultimately, if this is done well, they will have reliable access to optimal states of mind independent of their context. All schooling is an immersion in power structures and exchange processes that will shape the educational outcomes for everyone involved. The educational outcomes need to be measured, first, according to how reliably participants in the learning community access optimal states of mind across different contexts. Only after a baseline of reliable access to optimal states of mind has been established should the appropriate demonstration of symbol-manipulation skills by students be considered a central measure of the effectiveness of a course of study or a school.

Now consider the moral consequences of the trade-offs that society makes in the different kinds of schooling and the effects at a personal level for parents and their communities. Parents and their neighbors have no immediate concrete concern for society; the responsibility for the life of a single child is what occupies the vast majority of their attention. They know, love, and have a heartfelt obligation to provide the highest quality of life that they can manage for that child. Given that the whole continuum of schooling strategies (from froggish to human) is successful at providing for the perpetuation of society by producing productive citizens, then the true moral foundation of how to organize schooling hinges on which of the extremes should be preferred (or what balance to strike between them). This decision should be made based on the moral obligations of communities and families to individual children, since the perpetuation of society is already assured. Basically, society survives regardless of what choice you make, so the real moral issue is providing *your* child with the best opportunities for his or her success in life.

Neighbors and parents want good kids who grow up to be responsible, respectful, and resourceful adults. The community-level and family-level views of schooling reveal that preparation of young minds for the responsibilities of adulthood is the paramount concern. The challenge is to enable the child to make the crucial transition from a dependent person who relies on external authorities for behavioral management to becoming an *inter*dependent person who relies on an internalized network of mutual obligations (a.k.a. identities).

Behavioral management is a universal moral obligation; the question we always have to answer is how to control our own and other people's behavior for the common good. This question is answered in some way at all times; it is not a question we can ever evade. We inherently create power structures for this purpose. We are wired to defer to authority under most circumstances with just enough exceptions to hold the authorities accountable for keeping their personal egos and agendas from undermining the common good.

There is a continuum of authority. It ranges *from* the direct exercise of power based on the strong and bold getting their way (the authoritative behavior of an empowered individual over someone else within a particular situation) *to* the indirect exercise of power based on identity (the identification of a person with a group and the role that he or she is playing within a particular situation).

The other key element of how we organize behavioral management as a society, besides power structures, is the exchange processes that we use to meet our needs. The financial economy is the most obvious example of an exchange process we use. However, we exchange a lot more than just money in our lives. We exchange a great variety of things, including material resources, symbolic resources, and attention. Our current mainstream schooling system is organized around the exchanging of manipulated symbols and obedience to arbitrary authority.

Given the dictatorial level of power that teachers are given in the majority of classroom situations (even if they hate having to use that power), it is implicit that the baseline of what they will provide for children is a combination of instruction in symbol manipulation and training in obedience to arbitrary authority. The mainstream strategy is to throw as many symbol-manipulation activities at the kids as possible until eventually enough of them respond in the desired way to serve the purpose of perpetuating society. When the school system declares that someone has accrued all the right marks of instructional bookkeeping, they must be fit for adult society because that indicates their obedience to the symbol-manipulation requirements dictated by the system. (Note: This crass view of the system follows from the power structure, not from the behavior or attitudes of teachers. As I mentioned before,[22] teachers are not usually interested in being dictators because they realize how counterproductive applying such power is to deep learning.) However, traditional classroom schooling embodies a system that perpetuates dependence on direct control by authorities. The mainstream industrial classroom approach is handicapped by the absurd assumption that becoming a good citizen in a democratic society requires helping a child learn that the processes of exchanging manipulated symbols and obedience to direct authority are the most elementary factors of success in life.

Classroom instruction in symbol manipulation organized in this way may be causing a delay in the transition to internalized responsibility for mutual obligations. The primary developmental drive for humans is to understand how to achieve optimal states of mind within the social world in which they find themselves playing out some particular role. When children and their teachers are distracted from the primary developmental drive, the children's development may be delayed. The distraction is driven by the high stakes attached to performance in academic symbol-manipulation activities. They may also be distracted by the confusing blend of the teacher's authority to exercise behavioral control over students (as an official of the school) and their educational authority (as a fellow learner with more experience and knowledge of the field under study).

Unfortunately, every time a teacher exerts behavioral control, educational authority takes a back seat. When the students and teachers are all struggling to simultaneously juggle obedience challenges and academic-learning challenges, then academic-learning challenges will always get short shrift. Due to this fact, the mainstream system is extraordinarily wasteful of human energies, just like the reproductive strategies of frogs that are wasteful of individual offspring. In mainstream classrooms teachers scatter a great multitude of academic "eggs" in the vicinity of unprepared minds with the hope that a few of those "eggs" will randomly land in places where they can grow a child's mind in the direction of a deeper understanding of the world.

Democratic schools, by contrast, prepare young minds for nurturing whatever "eggs" will be carefully placed by the children in their own minds. The adults in the school know that in order for the children to attain and play out the roles that the children aspire to have as adults in society, they will need to incubate whatever eggs they acquire. Both strategies have proven to be generally effective at propagating society by producing productive citizens, though in the case of traditional classrooms, there is profligate waste of both resources and people. Democratic-school settings, on the other hand, are both efficient and effective.

Take, for example, what Daniel Greenberg has been doing for decades. He is one of the founders of the Sudbury Valley School that serves children aged four to nineteen years old in Framingham, Massachusetts. He teaches the entire first- through sixth-grade math curriculum with one hour a week of direct instruction over the course of twenty weeks to groups of children of any age who voluntarily sign up for the course.[23] For comparison, the State of Massachusetts expects publicly schooled children to attend a minimum of 180 days per school year[24] over six years with—let's assume—one hour each day devoted to math instruction. They anticipate children need somewhere near one thousand hours to learn the same curriculum Greenberg teaches in twenty—at least two orders of magnitude difference. Something fundamentally different is going on.

Democratic schools modeled after Sudbury Valley are organized to enable students to manage their own behavior and the day-to-day operations of the school. While there is a board that provides policy-level guidance and handles issues of legality, the students are the majority voters in the day-to-day operational decisions that determine the hiring of staff, the allocation of certain aspects of the budget, and every aspect of the establishment and enforcement of the rules of behavior. Each child has an equal opportunity to determine how resources are used. Other democratic schools vary in how much of the "adult" business of the school is accessible to the children. Some reserve for adults the final authority for decisions about hiring of staff, for instance.

Instructors in democratic schools are charged with answering to the explicitly expressed learning needs of the children and are not charged with the responsibility of being behavioral managers. I know this because I have volunteered for many years and was recently a contract instructor for a year at the Village Free School, a self-identified democratic school in Portland, Oregon. Behavioral management is accomplished by the democratic power structures and participatory exchange processes in which the students are embedded every day. The context for the instructional relationship is shaped by the fact that the students have both chosen to sign up for the class offering and authorized (even if indirectly) the hiring decision for each instructor. Instructional expectations are usually explicit and clear, but behavioral management is not a primary instructional duty. Instructors in democratic schools focus on their relationship with their students and their students' relationship with the subject at hand; behavioral control is the last thing on their mind.

Some instructors may also be teachers who are in attendance at the school for full- or part-time hours and may participate in the systems that manage behavioral issues, but that is regarded as separate from specific instructional duties. Teachers are charged by the students collectively (within policy guidance provided by the school's governing board) with a specific set of responsibilities for community leadership, not necessarily instruction.

What is missing from mainstream classroom schooling is proper facilitation of the transition from living with dependence on external control to living with dependence on an internalized system of mutual obligations defined by democratic participation in community governance. The transition I am referring to is that journey *from* being merely subject to authority *to* authorizing authorities and also becoming eligible to be a responsible agent of authority. The transition presumably occurs eventually in everyone who grows up to be a responsible adult, and it should normally occur in childhood. There is a developmental stage when children are discovering the social world beyond their family, and that seems like the best opportunity to inculcate democratic ideals. The transition would ideally occur between the ages of six and twelve. (Society has systematically ignored this possibility and succeeded nonetheless because the underlying biological drive will eventually precipitate some form of the transition in spite of whatever manipulations children are subjected to in schools.) In fact, what is necessary to facilitate the transition is enculturation in a system of mutual obligations.

The illusion that education can result from adults imposing academic activities on children's lives manifests itself most directly in the confusion between preparing young minds and controlling young people's behavior. The trouble is that a child's behavior is assumed to give the observer an approximate sense of the child's state of mind; thus, well-controlled behavior is also assumed to reflect a well-controlled state of mind. This is partly true, but in the very important ways that count for education, it is false.

The mind is far more complex than can be accounted for by simple observations of behavior. Directly observable behavior by a random stranger is a very shallow and inadequate indicator of any person's state of mind. (In the case of an observer who has a long term and intimate relationship with the person being observed, there can be a greater ability to correlate behavior with state of mind, but it is still not very reliable.) The trouble with judging the quality of a democratic school on the basis of the day-to-day activities of the children, as the media is wont to do, is that the actual learning processes are so efficient and effective that in a random sampling there is little chance that the particular moments of learning would be observed and even less chance that they would be recognized as such. The observer who expects to see adult-controlled mathematical activities at Sudbury Valley School is likely to be disappointed when there are two orders of magnitude less of them than the norm. The observable day-to-day activities in democratic schools should be considered the preparations of the mind for instruction, not an indication of instruction. What occurs on a day-to-day basis is a form of teaching that is concerned with the shaping of identity, expectations, and the enculturation to the power structures and exchange processes of the community. The subtle issues of identity, expectations, and enculturation ultimately determine the quality of the educational outcomes. The poor results that have been consistently observed in mainstream classrooms are the consequences of those subtler issues, not the obvious ones that the media usually blames.

Democratic schools are facilitating social development that serves to make the instruction that children actively choose for themselves an expression of their self-determined identity. The learning that follows from a person's own self-identification is going to tend to be deep rather than shallow. In order to fulfill the calling to systematically facilitate deeper learning in mainstream schools, the illusion about learning needs to be dispelled.

The primary obstacle blocking our way to an education system that truly fulfills our moral obligations to our children, society, and all of Life is the illusion that was operating when schools were designed for the mass, industrial-style production of obedient symbol manipulators. The flaw in the plan was not the industrial design process, which has been a very popular criticism of traditional classroom schooling for a century now. The fear behind the criticism of "industrial" schooling is that alienation, and worse harms, will follow from treating masses of people like things to be manipulated. That is a well-founded fear, and the evidence that it has been realized en masse is remarkably consistent. The alienation and other harms are exactly what is wrong with mass schooling, and it is inherent to how the froggish strategy works. But treating people that way is immoral, regardless of the scale and the ideology behind the design.

The flaw is that the system is designed to mass-produce obedient symbol manipulators when it should be mass-producing socially *inter*dependent state-of-mind optimizers. What if we can mass-produce well-being, leading to masses of motivated and engaged students and teachers who learn to collaboratively enhance each other's talents and gifts as they apply them to the most salient challenges facing their communities? If the critique of the "industrial system" is not merely ideological posturing, a convenient straw-man argument used for an emotional effect, then mass production of well-being as a means to facilitating deeper learning should be exactly what we are aiming for. Using industrial design tools and processes is exactly what we should do as long as using them can reliably produce that specific outcome.

The crucial framework for understanding how to shift our schooling system is morality. Morality is ultimately about well-being.[25] The larger challenge we face, even beyond schooling, is how to align our efforts to create well-being across many levels of reality. We are challenged to balance all human actions spanning from the global level, at which climate change is occurring, all the way down to the cellular level, at which disease and environmental toxicity have detrimental effects on our well-being. This is a spiritual challenge because it involves grappling with understanding and aligning our actions across scales of magnitude that we do not have any access to directly experiencing. This is spiritual in the sense that there are forces both within and outside of us that we are not normally aware of and that ultimately affect our well-being. Morality is our guide to achieving well-being, both individually and collectively, and we need to apply moral reasoning to the challenges that face us at this time.

Morality is about the imaginative application of principles that are ultimately intended to result in well-being; it is not about following rules.[26] Our moral quest today is to overcome our own limited conceptions of how the world works and to focus on taking actions that create well-being simultaneously for the cells within us and the entire planet that we depend upon for our existence. We have to weave together the strands of both science and religion to arrive at moral principles for taking action at all levels. And we need to judge the results on how well we facilitate the achievement of optimal states of mind through the creation of social systems that are engaging (as opposed to how well symbols are manipulated within weak social structures that tend to be alienating). It is time for maximizing human engagement at all levels of governance. We need to understand that governance is the monitoring and modification of the flows of energy and information through organizations and society. Notice that the previous statement implies that governance is how we "mind" organizations and society. Our only hope of addressing any of our problems sustainably is to transform governance at all levels into engaging processes in which citizens gladly participate. It is ultimately the widespread disengagement from governance itself that threatens the survival of our species. When we disengage from governance, then we are pushing our organizations and society toward mindlessness; that is not a good direction to be going in.

The tools of both science and religion can help. The term "religion" is based on a root that means "to bind together." We need to apply the scientific understanding of what causes engagement with the religious traditions that have proven to be so effectively engaging for so long. The legitimacy of organizations should be called into question if they promote passive membership, do not effectively work toward the well-being of all the individuals within their membership, or do not promote well-being for society as a whole, including people and all forms of life beyond their organizational boundaries. Organizations (religious and secular, scientific, or otherwise) need to be held accountable for maximizing the engagement of the people they affect. Organizations that fail to create productive engagement should be replaced by organizations that can, starting with schools.

Optimal states of mind as the legacy of life itself have some practical implications for our primary schools; they should lay off bombarding children with symbol-manipulation activities until the children have such good maps of their personal means of accessing optimal states of mind that they actively choose to receive instruction in manipulating symbols. At that point the children will be better able to efficiently incorporate the various symbol-manipulation activities into their growing repertoire of mind-optimizing strategies. Primary education also needs to take responsibility for helping children build ever-increasing skills for using power to simultaneously achieve their own and their community's goals.

The moral obligations of schools include making their power structures and exchange processes transparent. We cannot optimize something that we do not even know is there. When we make the power structures and exchange processes visible to everyone, then we can work with them. Every parent and child should be able to understand the connections between how the power to control people's behavior is wielded, how it can be changed, and how their participation in the decision-making process makes a difference in their own lives and the lives of others. How we protect the common good needs to be easy to see, evaluate, and correct, as necessary.

The education illusion is a major barrier to accomplishing the moral task ahead. As long as we distract children for years on end from the urgent task of tuning into their ability to access optimal states of mind, then we squander the most important tool God gave humanity for solving problems.

It is an illusion that causes us to believe that the behavioral control demonstrated in typical classrooms is universally beneficial to children. That same illusion leads some to judge the day-to-day behavior in democratic schools to be inappropriate for educational purposes. That illusion arises from an inherited gap in our understanding of the history of life. Once our short literate heritage is put into perspective as a continuation of our previously neglected long evolutionary heritage of optimizing states of mind in participatory social groups, then it is clear how the illusion arises. From the perspective of our deep history, we can see that symbol manipulation has become important, but it is only important within the context of achieving optimal states of mind. If symbol manipulation interferes with achieving optimal states of mind, then it has become counterproductive. Achieving optimal states requires responsible adults to facilitate the development of a strong internal social identity in every child that will encourage lifelong learning about their mutual obligations within their communities and more broadly the community of life.

The long-term goal of putting democracy in schools is to produce good citizens through encouraging skillful uses of power by all community members as they simultaneously pursue both their own and their community's goals. The short-term goal is optimizing states of mind. We cannot achieve the long-term goal if we consistently undermine the short-term goal by coercively maximizing the symbol-manipulation activities of our children. If we truly aspire to democracy, then we need to see schooling as the preparation for a democratic way of life. We cannot maintain a democratic way of life if we deny our children the experience of living democratically—of living within a governance system that is engaging rather than alienating. So let's give them the opportunity by reforming schools according to democratic principles derived from the psychology of engagement. Let's enable children to participate in making the decisions that affect them and in resolving conflicts through gatherings of mutually committed community members. Self-identified holistic and democratic schools have pioneered some useful methods, and every school community undoubtedly has strengths and traditions upon which they can build moving forward.

I am not advocating for a wholesale transition to democratic schooling in either Sudbury- or VFS-style, to Marietta Johnson–style organic education, or to universal homeschooling,[27] but I am advocating for the development of a systematic look at the power structures and exchange processes that shape the patterns of consciousness of students and teachers in every school. With that evaluation in hand, we should formulate plans for increasing the effective participation of students and teachers in the decisions that affect their activities most directly. Parents and teachers can lead the way by choosing to participate in the most democratic forms of schooling they can find or create, including homeschooling, if necessary. In addition to the terms "holistic" and "democratic," there are movements in this vein under the terms "deeper learning,"[28] "rights respecting schools,"[29] and probably others.

# Four

## Dispelling The Illusion

We are biological beings who have a four-billion-year heritage. That heritage gives us a limited range of moral options, but we do have a choice about how we are going to proceed. I suggest that what distinguishes the options available to us are our aesthetic judgments about what would serve goodness, truth, beauty, and joy.

We *could* continue to have schools that encourage self-fulfilling prophesies of apathy, mistrust, and disinterested behavior. We *could* continue to support systems of schooling that harbor bullies[30] and occasionally inspire worse violence. We *could* continue to make the offer that the little girl we met in the introduction rightly rejected.

Or we *could* tap both ancient and modern techniques for facilitating access to the great variety of ways we have found to optimize individual states of mind (including manipulating symbols). Using those techniques, we *could* cultivate the internal social identity of each child, encouraging a lifetime of deep learning directed toward striking the right balance between their personal goals and the goals of their community. We *could* encourage students and teachers to optimize their states of mind within democratic schools. We *could* offer seven-year-olds a new kind of schoolwork that embodies our democratic ideals instead of their opposites.

But *how*, you ask. I don't know. Well, I kinda know because of my experience with holistic schools and democratic schools, in particular. But I don't know how it would look in your particular community or school, though I can be pretty sure that however y'all put together a holistic school, it would share some design principles with the ones that have gone before. Let's explore a parallel example.

Our transportation system is probably the single most democratic institution in our society today. Think about how comprehensive it is. Just about anyone can get just about anywhere. From sidewalks to bicycles to jet airplanes, we empower people to self-determine their location without directly controlling them. We have a variety of ways to encourage them to make choices, both wise and unwise, with some thought to making the most common unwise choices minimally disruptive. But we don't presume to know where each person should go nor how they should get where they want to be.

Now, consider airports. There are lots of ways to build airports, but I don't know how y'all would build one in your particular community. I have no way of knowing what your transportation infrastructure already has in place and how your airport would need to fit into that context. But I can be confident that it will meet some design principles that would make it fit into the transportation system more broadly.

If airports were regulated like mainstream K–12 schools are currently, then everyone would be required to have travel agents who control where you go and how you get there. You would have new travel agents every year, and in the latter part of the process, the number of travel agents would expand from one or two in the elementary years to seven or more in high school. Universal standardization would be an obvious solution to the complexity of handling so many imposed itineraries. A massive bureaucratic and political nightmare would be the result, which happens to reflect the current reality in our K–12 education system, but not our transportation system.

The following table uses the airport analogy as a thought experiment to understand how holistic schools within our education ecology have similarities to airports within the transportation ecology. The left column takes the airport or transportation side, and the right column presents a parallel construction for school or education. The italics indicate the substantive changes between the two columns.

# Education Can *ONLY* Be Offered

| **Transportation System** | **Education System** |
|---|---|

## Guiding Question

How do *airports* (and the *transportation* system, more broadly) succeed at facilitating the *mobility* of multitudes of *people* every day without directly controlling their activities?

How do *holistic or democratic schools* (and *could* the *education* system, more broadly) succeed at facilitating the *education* of multitudes of *children* every day without directly controlling their activities?

## Units of analysis

*Travelers* (people *traveling*)

*Learners* (people *learning*)

*Travel* catalysts (*airport* service providers such as *airlines, cab companies, restaurants, travel agents, etc.*)

*Learning* catalysts (*school* service providers such as *teachers, food services, disability specialists, etc.*)

*Travel* context (*e.g., airports, government regulations, cities, and flying technologies*)

*Learning* context (*e.g., schools, tutoring services, camps, after-school programs, books, and cities*)

## Design principles

*Travelers* make their own decisions.

*Learners* make their own decisions (*within the contexts of their families and communities*).

*Travel* catalysts serve *travelers*.

*Learning* catalysts serve *learners*.

The *travel* context is designed to make the relationship between *travelers* and their chosen catalysts as easy as possible given certain minimum standards of health, safety, and fairness.

The *learning* context is designed to make the relationship between *learners* and their chosen catalysts as easy as possible given certain minimum standards of health, safety, and fairness (*including provisions for primary human-need support*).

| Transportation System | Education System |
|---|---|

## Design principles (continued)

Only the *traveler* is responsible for ensuring that they each have a *destination* and deciding how they should *get to their destination*.

Only the *learner* is responsible for ensuring they have *a goal* and deciding how they should *pursue their goal. (Keep in mind that all humans have some unconscious goals derived from their primary human needs for air, water, food, shelter, sleep, relatedness, competence, and autonomy and that children are assumed to be inescapably embedded in their family and the wider community.)*

The *travel* industry is made up of interlocking sets of organizations of people responsible for making sure that *travelers* have catalysts available to help them.

The *education* industry is made up of interlocking sets of organizations of people responsible for making sure that *learners* have catalysts available to help them. *(Ideally the education industry and its component organizations represent well-structured communities, discussed in more detail below this table.)*

The *port authority* is the organization of people responsible for ensuring that each *airport* is organized appropriately to facilitate the relationships between *travelers* and their chosen catalysts.

The *administrations of schools, districts, state education agencies, charter-granting agencies, or education-management organizations* are the organizations of people responsible for ensuring that each *school* is organized appropriately to facilitate the relationships between *learners* and their chosen catalysts.

## Transportation System | ## Education System

### Design principles (continued)

*Airport* management knows that the most important outcome is ensuring that all the *travelers* who choose to *fly into or out of that airport* have the ability to find their way through the system in pursuit of their own goals.

*School* management knows that the most important outcome is ensuring that all the *learners* who choose to *attend that school* have the ability to find their way through the system in pursuit of their own goals.

Service providers within the *airport* are presumed to be experts on what they do to further the *travelers'* goals.

Service providers (*teachers or other activity facilitators*) within the *school* are presumed to be experts on what they do to further the *learners'* goals.

Enabling *travelers* to achieve their goals is the primary gauge of success for service providers (via autonomous choices within a regulated service-provider market. A market in the *broader* sense that *travelers* have real choices about how to pursue their goals and aspirations, not *just* in a monetary-exchange sense).

Enabling the *learners* to achieve their goals is the primary gauge of success for service providers (via autonomous choices within a regulated service-provider market. A market in the sense that *children* have real choices about how to pursue their goals and aspirations, not in a monetary-exchange sense).

The service providers rely on the *airport* to enable them to communicate with *travelers* in a variety of ways so that the *travelers* can make good decisions (via signage *and other forms of information distribution.*)

The service providers rely on the *school* to enable them to communicate with *learners* in a variety of ways so that the *learners* can make good decisions (via signage, *newsletters, course catalogs, etc.*)

The service providers also enable the *travelers* to adjust their decisions on the fly as either the situation changes or they discover that they have made a mistake.

The service providers also enable the *learners* to adjust their decisions on the fly as either the situation changes or they discover that they have made a mistake.

All children and adults need access to nurturing within a community support system. Holistic schools, including the democratic ones that I have focused on, are designed to provide that. Too many children do not have equitable access to such a system. The effectiveness of adults charged with nurturing responsibilities should be evaluated in light of data on the well-being, motivation, and engagement of their students. Society cannot know whether or not adults have met their moral obligations if they do not have reasonably objective information about those psychological aspects of their students' experiences.[31] The design criteria in the table above can serve as a principled guide to where we want to end up, with a well-structured education system.

Well-structured communities are the key to sustainable success. In well-structured communities, mistakes are accepted as a normal part of being in community for both adults and children. Well-structured communities continue to function no matter who makes a mistake. Mistakes are taken as opportunities to be more supportive, not less. Communities can be well-structured both within their organizational boundaries and as part of the overlapping sets of organizations that make up the industry. Education includes families, schools, businesses, government agencies, and civil society (NGO's or nonprofits). Having a multitude of individuals and organizations serving critical functions at each level ensures that there will be support provided even if some of the individuals or organizations fail or make mistakes.

Equitable access to educational opportunities and resources is important. Equitable access would be one of the key criteria for discerning the quality of the structure of a community. Judgments of whether access is absent or inequitably present should start with an analysis of how well supported primary human needs are across the population before other considerations are included. For instance, the disparities in scores on standardized tests that appear to be based on race or any other oppression indicator are not currently solvable equity issues. This insolvability is because of the pervasive lack of primary human need support for the children who are subjected to the tests. The organizations representing traditionally oppressed populations that have called for compliance with the testing mandates are well intentioned but mistaken in their support for compliance. The central equity issue they should be focused on is access to primary human need support in schools, not academic support. Research shows that primary need support improves academic outcomes, so this is a matter of getting both, not one to the exclusion of the other.[32]

Another example of an equity issue being misunderstood is that of standards. Standards are great, but only for those who choose to meet them. We do not make everyone become a doctor, but when someone chooses to become a doctor, then he or she is simultaneously choosing to meet professional standards. Imposing standards universally should be carefully reserved for instances that have the potential for tragedy such as public-health measures for controlling communicable diseases, the structural safety of bridges and buildings, and supporting primary human needs. Enforcing universal academic standards on *children* is *not* necessary. But enforcing universal standards for supporting primary human needs in *schools* may be *essential.*

The challenge of education should be met in a democratic society in a democratic manner. The undemocratic character of schooling undermines democracy. We need to offer our seven-year-olds schoolwork that is empowering and in a manner that promotes their well-being, not diminishes it. I suspect most, perhaps all, holistic schools are leading the way, but I know that democratic schools are doing so because there are data to that effect (and I produced some of it).[33] I am comfortable extrapolating from that small sample of data for both theoretical and political reasons.

As a psychologist I have studied motivation and its relationship to learning. The science is clear and consistent that motivation is crucial to deeper learning. If we can better support primary human needs in schools, we will get better well-being. Better well-being will improve motivation. When we get improved motivation, we will get more engagement. Better engagement will produce deeper learning. I refer you to my previous book, *Most Schools Won't Fit: Every Parent's Dilemma and What to Do About It*, coauthored with parent Holly Allen, for a brief guide to psychological need support and providing appropriate structure.[34] For greater depth I recommend Jennifer Fredricks's book *Eight Myths of Disengaged Students: Creating Classrooms of Deep Learning.*[35]

My thoughts on psychology become political at this point because getting deeper learning to be more widespread is the only hope we have of solving our global challenges like poverty, disengaged citizens, environmental destruction, and so on. The psychological becomes political when we have to translate what we know about well-being into societal systems that distribute decision-making opportunities through a power structure.

We need to train our children in making decisions, not merely how to live with the consequences of someone else's decisions. We need to organize our schools to provide the optimal environment for them to engage with governance in order to learn that good governance is one of the most important prerequisites to achieving their goals and aspirations. They need to live through the challenges of making real, meaningful decisions and living with the consequences of those decisions at a time in their life when the consequences are, from our adult perspective, small and less impactful on others. The children will not share our perspective; they will have the sense that a large magnitude of effect on their lives will result from choosing whether their school should ban, limit, or supply Legos, collectible card games, mobile devices, power tools, or whatever. Whether each decision has that degree of impact or not is irrelevant. Actively participating in making those decisions repeatedly is how they learn the real ins and outs of governance. It is their engagement in the process and living with the consequences of collective decisions that provides them with the experience of what it means to live in a democratic society. That is what is missing in mainstream schools but is supplied in abundance in holistic schools. My political agenda is to get holism to be a feature of more schools.

While the airport analogy gives us principled outcomes to aim for, we still need to be able to examine what is currently the case. In the following section, I lay out a framework for examining how we play out our roles in organizations. Taking optimal states of mind to heart means we have to view all of our activities from that perspective. The Attitutor Participation Map is a lens that can help us focus on how our roles contribute to optimizing states of mind across the levels of the individual, the organization, and society.

# Mapping the Power of Participation

Every person is an agent; they have agency to act. The overarching goal of their actions, independent of all other factors, is to optimize their state of mind. The challenge is how to arrange organizations and society to better enable humans to have lives that have a consistently high level of quality. The Attitutor Participation Map provides participants in organizations with guidelines for achieving higher quality outcomes more consistently. That happens when they have consistent access to optimal states of mind.

*CORE OF THE PARTICIPATION MAP: AGENTS OPTIMIZING STATES OF MIND*
Given the assumption that optimizing states of mind is a universal goal, organisms can always be counted on to

1. solve problems, where problems are conditions that cause nonoptimal states of mind and attempts to solve them result in changes to states of mind, and
2. pursue goals, where goals are experiments in optimizing states of mind and pursuing them means initiating and maintaining activities in order to access or retain optimal states.

For humans there is a third universal activity when they are part of a group: playfully having fun.[36] When a person joins a group, they would naturally expect group participation to provide more access to optimal states of mind than not participating (without being conscious of that expectation). So, within the context of a group, each person will desire to playfully have fun,[37] where playful fun is expected to be cooperative experiments in simultaneously optimizing the states of mind of everyone in the group.

Naturally, experiments are not necessarily successful, so expectations are not always met. But the ultimate goal of accessing optimal states of mind does not change even though the conditions in which it is pursued and the results that occur can and do vary widely. The inherent outcome of all activities is learning, whether or not we are aware of having learned. At a minimum we learn that our current model of the world still seems to be good enough for now. For this model, the terms "agent" and "learner" are equivalent when referring to humans. Today the prototypical learner is probably a student, and the prototypical student is probably a child or youth. However, there is no reason to limit the application of this model to those prototypes.

The typical image of a classroom is one in which there is an active teacher and passive students.[38] This image is grossly misleading when it is used to guide the design and management of schools. The "learner" in this image does not inherently display any of the characteristics that psychologists have found contribute to the deeper learning that is necessary in today's global society.

In order to imagine what this learner-as-agent model implies, I suggest you envision the enthusiastic engagement of a child with an object that incites wonder and a passion for finding out more about it. That is probably a lot easier to do if you imagine that child engaged in something outside of school. Think of something that they would have chosen for themselves and can do without adults in control of the situation.

If you grew up in an area or an era in which children were free to roam the neighborhood and self-determine their activities and the company they kept, then you can probably imagine something that is appropriate. If you didn't grow up that way, then I suggest you think about movies or TV shows that depict kids in situations in which they are self-directed. Even in the highly institutionalized setting of the imaginary Hogwarts boarding school, you can see self-directed learning at play. Consider the student-made Marauder's Map, all of the gag novelties created by the twins Fred and George Weasley, and how much creative energy went into subverting adult authority, especially in Dumbodore's Army. Can you imagine a school in which those energies were supported instead of thwarted? Instead of creating arbitrarily restrictive structures that children resent, what if we create an organizational structure in which they actively participate in the re-creation and adjustment of governance itself?

Matthew Appleton, a former staff person at A. S. Neill's Summerhill School in the United Kingdom, wrote about how the children there occasionally take advantage of their power to abolish all the rules.[39] It is a boarding school, so, naturally, where the children have a significant impact on each other some degree of chaos ensues, e.g. around bedtimes and other aspects of the day-to-day life of the school. On the occasion he recounted, the rule book was soon reconstructed from scratch. That might be the ultimate lesson in democratic governance. (I recommend the BBC's dramatization of the government attempt to shut Summerhill down if you would like a fun way to see a little bit more about how the school works.)[40]

Can you imagine the possibility of a school being structured in a way that enabled students to make changes to suit their collective and individual needs? Unfortunately, visualizing schools that are so different from the mainstream is difficult, and we have a dearth of media that portray models of well-functioning governance to make it easier.

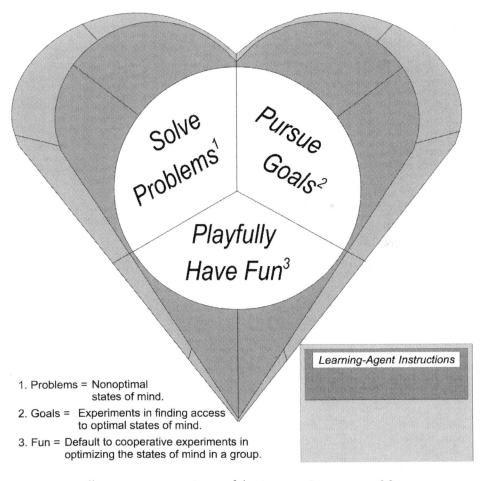

*Learning-Agent Instructions*

1. Problems = Nonoptimal states of mind.
2. Goals = Experiments in finding access to optimal states of mind.
3. Fun = Default to cooperative experiments in optimizing the states of mind in a group.

Illustration 1: Agent Layer of the Attitutor Participation Map

Solving problems, pursuing goals, and playfully having fun are the three actions that form the inner core of the participation map shown in illustration 1. The rest of the map is about how we could spot or create organizations that would fulfill the requirements for supporting the optimization of states of mind.

The quality of learning in a given situation for an individual can be judged by the degree to which optimal states were accessed and how easy or difficult it is to re-create that degree of access in the future. To paraphrase John Dewey, finding access to optimal states of mind now is the best preparation for finding access to optimal states of mind in the future. This provides us with the element that is necessary to fulfill Dewey's call for a theory of experience that will allow us to evaluate the educative benefits of individual learning.[41] But the nature of this model requires further evaluation of the effectiveness of the organization.

There are two more layers to the map that provide insight into how organizations function to support individuals in their pursuit of optimal states of mind. Another way of thinking about it is to say that the other two layers inform us about how individuals function as the mind of the organization—that is, how crucial flows of energy and information are managed for a group.

*MIDDLE LAYER OF THE PARTICIPATION MAP: CATALYSIS OF OPTIMAL STATES OF MIND*

As a member of any group, an individual has access to resources that catalyze learning. A literal catalyst is a chemical that facilitates a reaction between other chemicals without being changed by the reaction it facilitates. What is necessary for a catalyst in the school sense to be an effective learning tool is for the learner to focus sufficient attention on the catalyst such that their mental maps are actively engaged in the process of experiencing the catalyst. Learning catalysts might prototypically be thought of as teachers, but almost anything can serve. Most importantly, the attention allocations of the learner determine the level of influence that a learning catalyst will have. When the catalysts are human and they are operating within the auspices of an organization, then they have the responsibility to act, individually or collectively, in two distinct roles: the intimate catalyst and the organizational catalyst.

In the role of *intimate catalyst*, an individual acts with and for other agents to facilitate learning (independent of their awareness of doing so). In order to support the primary psychological needs of the agents within the organization, intimate catalysts should be

- encouraging empathy and empathizing in order to support the development of relatedness,
- planning ahead in order to support the development of competence, and
- facilitating decision making in a manner that supports autonomy.

You should notice that these aspects of the map are specifically directed towards supporting three of the primary human needs.

Since competence cannot be magically bestowed by another and we cannot reliably read minds, it is important that the development of competence includes a substantial amount of input from the learners. This leads to the principle that planning must be shared with learners to ensure that their input is instrumental in guiding the process.

Supporting autonomy in decision making is most likely to be achieved by delegating each decision to the lowest possible level within the organization. Thus this aspect of the intimate-catalyst layer calls for distribution of decision making. This is also what many people might call being democratic, though that label is not important.

An *organizational catalyst* embodies the roles of technician, manager, and entrepreneur. These are basic functional roles in organizations drawn from the book *The E-Myth* by Michael Gerber. A technician in a school is a person who is attending to the finest level of details of making basic outcomes happen for the learning agents. A manager is a person attending to the immediate needs of the organization in relation to the people and other organizations that contribute to the organization's survival. And an entrepreneur is a person who attends to both the long-term functioning within the organization and to the changes in the world beyond the organization. An entrepreneur enables the organization to change in ways appropriate to foreseeable alterations in its context. These roles can all be enacted by any members of the organization, independent of their awareness of doing so. Organizations might be wise to assign responsibility for them to specific individuals, but even then their actual function can still be fulfilled by anyone who has the opportunity and acts on it (once again, regardless of being aware of it or not).

The catalyst layer of the map (illustration 2) is the inner heart shape that directly surrounds the circular core. I chose the heart shape because the catalysts are directly responsible for nurturing the agents in the organization.

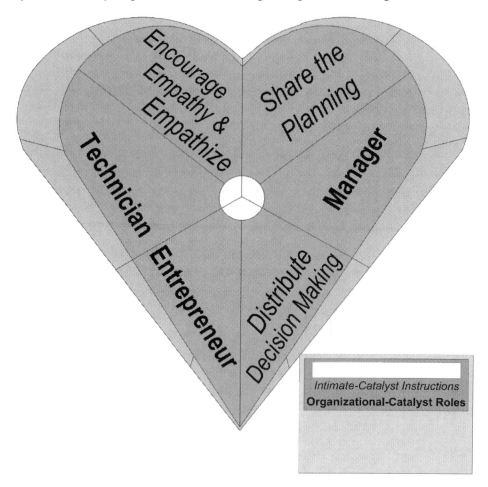

Illustration 2: Catalyst Layer of the Attitutor Participation Map

*OUTER LAYER OF THE PARTICIPATION MAP: A CONTEXT OF SUPPORT FOR OPTIMAL STATES OF MIND*

The context of a group also requires people to take action on behalf of the organization. The context layer is the outer heart shape in the map. I kept the heart shape because, in order for the catalysts to be nurturing, the context also has to be structured to support nurturing behaviors. If the context is structured in a manner that thwarts nurturing, the catalysts will be undermined, as the current state of the mainstream K–12 school system demonstrates. A reasonable prototype of a person responsible for the learning context in education is the school principal, originally known as the school's principal teacher. Once again, it is not necessary to limit the application of the concept to the prototype. Also, note that everyone in an organization contributes to the context, even without knowing it. Individuals actively taking responsibility for the organization (as a learning context in which learning agents and learning catalysts relate to each other) must collectively think and act at three levels of scale for the organization: at the level of an intimate context, at the level of an organizational context, and at the level of a societal context. Context is the realm of factors in the relationship between agents and catalysts that are most often not within their awareness—factors such as language, architecture, cultural traditions, furnishings, scheduling, use of space, and so on. The learning context is partly the realm in which policies in the broadest sense are used as a mechanism for managing the behaviors of the organization's members.

For the *intimate context*, the responsible parties must encode

- respect,
- responsibility, and
- resourcefulness.

The following definitions translate these terms from the language of virtues[42] into six components of optimal states of mind using terms from positive psychology. The six components of optimal states of mind are increasing cognitive complexity, negotiating cooperation, ordering consciousness, enhancing agency, acting on purpose, and reinforcing optimism.[43] I consider the six components to describe ranges in which a mind operating at the extremes of the range will experience nonoptimal states while the appropriate balance between the extremes results in optimality. The ranges can be mapped as a state space for the mind. The extremes of the ranges are defined by over reliance on information sourced from the self or others. The conditions for optimality can and do change; optimality is a moving target. For each balanced state, I have created two labels that I think are apt for each of the unbalanced states, as well:

**The New 3R's with Associated Psychological Components Table**

| | Respect | | Responsibility | | Resourcefulness | |
|---|---|---|---|---|---|---|
| **Too Self Determined** | Chaotic | Slavish | Bored | Isolated Independence | Obsessive | Pessimistic: Disengaged Action |
| **Balanced State of Mind** | Complex | Cooperative | Ordered | Agentic | Purposeful | Optimistic |
| **Too Other Determined** | Simplistic | Tyrannical | Distracted | Blind Obedience or Groupthink | Spiritual Hunger | Cynical: Resigned Passivity |

Respect is about seeing people or situations again (*re-*, again; *-spect*, to see). When we are being respectful, we make it a habit to take a different perspective, especially to see other people's points of view, before we make decisions or take actions that might affect them. A proper practice of respect provides robust opportunities for developing cognitive complexity and negotiating cooperation.

Responsibility is about altering our ability to respond (*respons-*, to respond; *-ibility*, ability). It is not reasonable to expect that our habitual ways of responding are capable of gracefully and appropriately handling every situation that we will encounter from now on; therefore we need to continuously adjust our repertoire. A proper practice of responsibility provides robust opportunities for developing cognitive order and enhancing agency.

Resourcefulness is about being full of our source again. Two important sources that we should be full of are the Earth as our material source and the Mystery (a.k.a. God, Allah, Goddess, etc.) as our ultimate source. The sources are metaphorical allusions to the inherent dependence we have on the hidden aspects and forces that influence us in both the inner and outer worlds. A proper practice of resourcefulness provides robust opportunities for acting on purpose and reinforcing optimism.

In this view the three Rs are states of mind that are drawn out of the individuals who make up the organization. The situation created by any given organization elicits a range of behaviors. These virtues are neither stable dispositions of individuals nor qualities that individuals have complete volitional control over. When a situation produces a nonoptimal state, then the situation needs to be examined for ways that it may be contributing to the states of mind that occur. Individuals are still culpable for the results of their behavior, but the situational factors need to be addressed as well.

For the *organizational context*, the responsible parties must ensure that the group has a participatory structure, fair process, and profitable pattern. The additional parenthetical labels in the table are explained below.

| | |
|---|---|
| Participatory Structure (Human capital) | A system of management that gives all the affected agents (or stakeholders) an explicit role to play in the making of decisions that affect their lives. |
| Fair Process (Relational capital) | Having explicit methods for restoring relationships within the organization after they have been disrupted by conflict. |
| Profitable pattern (Decisional capital) | Ensuring management of organizational income and assets systematically provides for both current and foreseeable future needs with enough leeway to handle some unforeseeable circumstances as well. (Notice that this is profitable in a broad sense, not in the narrow capitalist financial sense.) |

Individuals fulfilling the obligations of the organizational context or organizational catalyst are ensuring that the organization has an active mind; they are acting as the process for monitoring and modifying flows of energy and information through the organization (including but not limited to finances).

For another perspective on the same level of concern, I refer you to the book *Professional Capital* by Andy Hargreaves and Michael Fullan.[44] The book is about how to be an effective school principal. Remember that this school title was derived from the archaic phrase "principal teacher," and for my purpose here, it is a title that applies to those who take responsibility for the context that the organization collectively creates.

Hargreaves and Fullan organize their take on educational leadership in terms of various forms of capital that need to be developed. They seem to have taken their cue from the idea of developing business capital in order to run a profitable enterprise. In business terms in order to accomplish certain kinds of tasks, you need access to a bunch of cash and other resources that are labeled "capital." Using this "capitalist" model, Hargreaves and Fullan talk about enabling the school organization to develop access to certain kinds of characteristics or properties in people which are necessary resources for the school organization to accomplish its purpose. They did not reference self-determination theory, but I see how their ideas neatly map onto primary human needs and the model developed here.

The support of relatedness is what Hargreaves and Fullan call the development of relational capital. The position of a principal teacher is often a highly political one in which there are competing constituencies that demand attention—parents, board members, district administrators, teachers, students, and so on. If the principal does not take time to develop relationships with key members of those groups, then when the chips are down, he or she will not be able to get things done effectively. The challenge is not how to operate when times are good. Where the rubber meets the road is when things get difficult.

Competence is what they call the development of human capital. The basic idea is that you can't get things done unless your workforce has skills that are appropriate to your business. Any group of humans will have lots of knowledge, skill, and information, but that doesn't matter unless the people you recruited have the right set that is needed for the challenges that are relevant to your organization. They have to be able to access them and have whatever support they need to use them appropriately, as well. In the democratic school I studied, I had previously volunteered in the office. Kelly and Jeva (not their real names), students who were each about ten years old, expressed interest in helping with office duties, answering phones in particular. The school phone is crucial to the business functions of outreach, recruiting, enrollment, and retention of students. In order to ensure that the business function would not be disrupted by their learning process, I devised a method of training them through simulations and practice so that their human capital could be developed without putting the business at risk. This kind of openness to student participation in any area of the school seems to be a common characteristic of democratic schools. They develop human capital throughout the school, even though they may not call it that.

The support of autonomy is what Hargreaves and Fullan call the development of decisional capital. If the teachers do not have the opportunity to make certain kinds of decisions on a regular basis, then they cannot develop the habits they need to make good decisions under difficult circumstances. The failure to make good decisions under difficult circumstances can be the death knell of a school or any organization. If, on the other hand, the leaders find ways to enable meaningful decision making to happen on a regular basis, then when hard times come, the skills are already primed and ready to go. You can see how decisional capital is developed in democratic schools through constant attention to making decisions about relationships in both conflict-resolution procedures and in rule-making and enforcement processes.

What Hargreaves and Fullan did, without apparently realizing it, was to reframe the primary human needs in different language. The goal of developing all three forms of capital is professionalism. So that is another way of characterizing what this level of the map is about. Playfulness may not be the most appropriate thing to talk about in the more adult-oriented organizational context, so professionalism is a good substitute. When all three forms of capital are developed together, you are supporting all three primary psychological needs and then what you get in adults is professionalism. Kids play, and adults act professionally. And professionalism properly understood is just an adult version of playfulness that is directed toward minding the organization.

For the *societal context*, responsible parties must strive to ensure enoughness, exchangeability, and common benefit. These three properties are drawn from Shariff Abdullah's book *Creating a World That Works For All*.

| Enoughness | Everyone having adequate resources to meet his or her primary needs. |
|---|---|
| Exchangeability | Ensuring that all the stakeholders could switch places with any other stakeholder and not have their ability to meet their primary needs compromised (even if they would prefer not to switch). |
| Common Benefit | When every aspect of the society is designed to provide value for those involved, then there is no one in the society who is being systematically disadvantaged by playing out their role (no scapegoats). |

Individuals fulfilling the obligations of the societal context are ensuring that the society has an active mind; they are acting as the process for monitoring and modifying flows of energy and information through the society. In the excerpt below from an opinion piece lamenting the lack of media coverage of junior-high and high-school activism, the writer cites a survey that shows that a significant percentage of schools were disrupted in the late '60s.

[H]igh school activism has taken place in almost every major U.S. city, as well as in some suburban and rural areas. It has occurred in public, private, parochial and boarding schools. In 1969, the National Association of Secondary School Principals surveyed more than 1,000 public and private school principals about social unrest in secondary schools. The survey revealed that 56 percent of junior high schools and 59 percent of high schools reported disturbances.[45]

The following quote from NPR covers more recent activism.

The Common Core-aligned Smarter Balanced exams, Elijah was told, were grueling .... [T]he only thing compelling Elijah to take the tests this past spring was No Child Left Behind, the federal law. ...

"If there's something you might risk failing but, regardless, you'll learn something or you'll be stronger because of it ... that's great," Elijah said in April as he organized a boycott of the tests at his school. "But if there's not a real benefit to passing or failing, then it's not worth it."

When testing day finally arrived in high schools across Washington, Elijah was one of more than 42,000 11th-graders — roughly half of the state's junior class — who did not show up for their exams. At least 22,000 of them formally refused to test. Many of the rest were AWOL.[46]

Elijah and his compatriots were making the case for their assessments to be meaningful contributions to their education, not worthless gestures of obedience to bureaucratic authority. Elijah and all the young activists from the '60s represent the possibility that teenagers can act as the conscience of our society just as capably as any adult can. They were taking action to reshape the context of schooling. The context is the outer layer of the participation map and is shown in illustration 3.

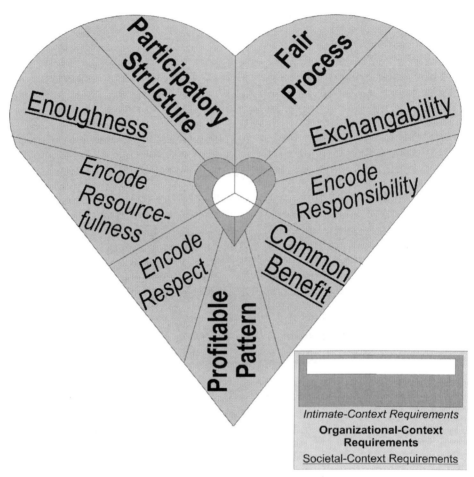

Illustration 3: Context Layer of the Attitutor Participation Map

The complete Attitutor Participation Map, presented in illustration 4, depicts guidelines for how organizations can best interact with their agents to be mutually supportive. It depicts a set of guidelines for school operations. It encompasses the support of primary human needs in a variety of ways, even though the needs are not displayed explicitly. The layers and elements of the participation map are not intended to be taken as representing distinctions that have any kind of material manifestations. The layers and elements are useful as conceptual tools about aspects of the unified whole that constitutes the organization.

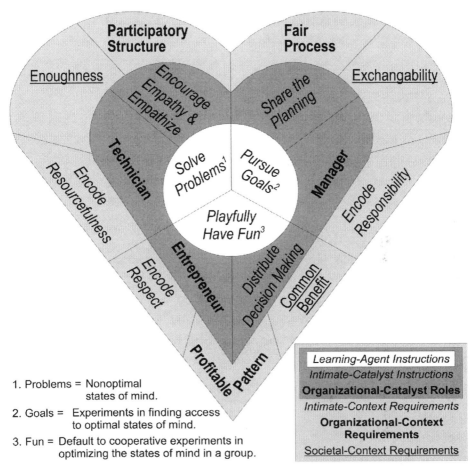

1. Problems = Nonoptimal
      states of mind.
2. Goals = Experiments in finding access
      to optimal states of mind.
3. Fun = Default to cooperative experiments in
      optimizing the states of mind in a group.

Learning-Agent Instructions
Intimate-Catalyst Instructions
**Organizational-Catalyst Roles**
Intimate-Context Requirements
**Organizational-Context
Requirements**
Societal-Context Requirements

Illustration 4: Attitutor Participation Map

# Using the Attitutor Participation Map

The Attitutor Participation Map suggests some easily accessible informal evaluations that may be helpful to parents and other members of a school organization. The most accessible are the three Rs of respect, responsibility, and resourcefulness. According to both *The Family Virtues Guide* and *Character Strengths and Virtues: A Handbook and Classification,* the three Rs are virtues that are universally taught in all human societies. Any adult can make an intuitive assessment of whether a school or classroom embodies respect, responsibility, and resourcefulness. It may not be the most scientifically valid assessment, but it is one that I would recommend to current or prospective members of a school community, especially parents who have the opportunity to select the school their child will attend.

The Attitutor Participation Map is experientially centered. What do I need to do? I need to solve problems, pursue goals, and playfully have fun. Those three tasks are always the prime directives for us humans, whether we know it or not. This set of directives is the grand strategy we have been given or evolved to have for pursuing the goal of optimizing states of mind. How are the agents in this environment solving problems, pursuing their goals, and playing fully to have fun? How well does the organization facilitate the integration of individual and organizational problems and goals? How well does the organization support the optimization of states of mind among both its members and itself?[47] How do we operate within our organization to optimize states of mind in a long-term, sustainable way?

The outer layer of the Attitutor Participation Map deals with the hidden curriculum: the inherent consequences of being embedded in an organization. All organizations create situations in which their members interact. The context that the organization creates will restrict the ranges of behavior that the agents will consider to be possible, acceptable, and desirable (with the resulting conceptions differing somewhat across individuals).

This map suggests a change in our habitual inquiry into behavioral problems from "How did the individuals fail in this situation?" to "How did the organization fail to support the individuals in this situation?" The first phase of an inquiry into problematic behavior should be concerned with primary human needs. Pursuit of primary needs is a baseline expectation for all agents. When the context thwarts or neglects primary-need satisfaction, this will have predictable negative effects. Dropping out, failing to achieve, and fauxchieving are predictable negative effects of neglecting or thwarting the primary psychological needs of students in schools. Stress, burnout, and turnover are also predictable negative effects of neglecting or thwarting the primary psychological needs of teachers in schools. (Rates of these phenomena will probably never be reduced to zero due to nonpsychological factors that produce the same results.)

If we are confronting behavioral problems, then we need to enable both the organization and the individuals involved to take responsibility for the situations that were regarded as problematic. All the individuals need to see responsibility as shared. There are both individual and collective opportunities to do something differently in response to problems that arise. There is *no less* responsibility for an individual when we recognize that the organization or society also played a role in causing the situation to happen. Acknowledging that society helped make a situation difficult does not absolve anyone of responsibility for their behavior. Individuals always have some degree of autonomy; they have some level of competence (even if it is a low level), and they have relationships that have to be taken into account. Society and organizations are not capable of taking responsibility for those facets of the situation. Those are forever and always an individual responsibility. Society and organizations can and do need to take responsibility for many of the aspects beyond those, particularly for how primary human needs are supported or not.

After primary needs, the context will have the most significant influence on behavior. The relationships that matter are among the learning agents, learning catalysts, and the context. The context determines the range of possibilities for the relationship between the agents and the catalysts. The challenge is to be able to understand past and present behavior and have a reasonable range of expectations regarding future behavior. One of the ways that cognitive psychology has challenged our view of how human minds work is to call into question the widespread view that people have fixed characteristics that they bring into situations, a view that is called dispositionism. The truth is that people have no specific characteristics that cannot be changed in response to some situations.[48] They have stable primary needs, they are embedded in complex multilayered situations (parts of which are also stable), and they seek stable patterns of participation in the organizational contexts that they occupy. The undeniable stability and consistency we normally experience in ourselves and others are largely a consequence of the stability and consistency of both our needs and the large-scale cultural and societal patterns in which we are embedded. This puts a very high degree of responsibility on those who create the situations that people occupy.[49]

In K–12 schools the responsible people include education practitioners; they need narrative frameworks, such as policies and procedures that specify particular protocols, to ensure that they meet the minimum standards of care for the children they are taking responsibility for educating. The challenge is to be able to describe the effective and ineffective approaches and strategies in appropriately admirable or critical terms regardless of whether the systems are informal or formal.

# Conclusion

## MAKING A BETTER OFFER

How do you imagine a seven-year-old would respond to this job offer?

- Your job is to solve problems, pursue goals, and playfully have fun.
- You will not earn a salary or receive financial-ownership shares in this organization, but by participating in our community, you will invest your time and energy in ways that will pay off for the rest of your life.
- Your power to make decisions as part of a community is one of the most important skills we can help you develop. We will help you understand and use your power for good and discourage you from turning evil. And with your help, we will stay good, too.
- When you make mistakes, or are hurt by someone else's mistake, we will provide more support, not less. We will help to heal the relationships disrupted by conflict and build both your skills and ours for resolving those problems and avoiding them in the future.
- We will provide you with abundant opportunities to participate in a democratic system for altering the decision-making processes that create and maintain all of these awesome ways to participate in being a part of our organization.

Schools that make this kind of offer should recognize themselves as part of their larger communities too. They are offering the opportunity to live in the kind of participatory community that makes our democratic society work. This is how I imagine the offer that holistic schools, generally, and democratic schools, in particular, are making to students might look.

Mainstream schools are a far cry from making this type of offer, but there are signs that many mainstream-school folks are interested in moving in this direction. The various calls or movements for deeper learning, Glasser quality schools, Comer schools, microschools, International Baccalaureate schools, twenty-first-century skills, and many other innovations that take into account (whether deliberately or by accident) the support of the primary psychological needs of the learners may be steering themselves down good paths. They should consider how they can distinguish psychologically well-founded practices from those that merely seem to be.

Schools that would like to move themselves away from the froggish end of the strategy spectrum can use the design principles and the Attitutor Participation Map as tools to move in that direction. Democratic and other holistic schools can use these ideas to better explain themselves and how they work in comparison to the mainstream. The more we can tell this story, the more schools will take an interest in moving in the right direction.

# Notes

1. This offer was inspired by Stanislav Shalunov's Blog Post "Would you work with micromanaging boss, no salary, and all your work thrown away?" Posted June 18, 2008, http://blog.shlang.com/post/38977434/ would-you-work-with-micromanaging-boss-no-salary

2. Berg and Corpus (2013).

3. AEE (n.d.), AIR & Hewlett Foundation (n.d.), Atherton (2013), Bellanca (2015), Berry (2016), Dunleavy and Milton (2010), Entwhistle (2003), Fullan and Quinn (2016), Kim (2015), Kysilko (2014), Martinez (2014), Mehta and Fine (2015), Miller, Latham, and Cahill (2017); NASBE (n.d.), NPDL (n.d.), Robinson and Aronica (2016), Trilling (2014), Washor and Mojkowski (2014), Zhao (2009).

4. The other five components of nurturing are air, water, food, shelter, and sleep.

5. NCES (National Center for Education Statistics) (2016).

6. Nord et al. (2011).

7. Gardner (2004).

8. Tyack (1974), Tyack and Cuban (1995).

9. "Dictatorial" describes the nature of the situation, not the nature of those who happen to be in it. I know that teachers and other well-meaning school folks bristle at my use of the term due to the negative connotations it has. Most adults in schools are benevolent in both their intentions and their actions, so the negative connotations of their assigned dictatorial powers can feel personally denigrating. But their understandable concern

does not change the fact that it is an accurate view of the situation they occupy, even when it is also an inaccurate *personal* characterization.

10. Dirkswager, Farris-Berg, and Junge (2012).

11. Berg and Corpus (2013).

12. IDEA (2012).

13. How Long Does a Female Frog Keep Eggs Inside Her Body? (n.d.).

14. My previous book *Most Schools Won't Fit* written with Holly Allen covers this topic. Berg and Allen (2017).

15. See http://www.SelfDeterminationTheory.org

16. See endnote 3 above.

17. Gallup (2016), Hastings and Agrawal (2015).

18. Marks (2000), Miller et al. (2017); The author estimates 65to 75% based on starting with a population of 58 million students then assuming that (1) 5.90% will drop out = 3.42 million (NCES, 2016), (2) 25% of the remainder will graduate below basic standards (Nord et al., 2011) = 13.46 million, and (3) 50 to 80% of the remainder will have been disengaged at a crucial point as noted by Gardner (2004) = 20.20 to 26.25 million. Thus, 37.08 to 43.13 million students, a range of 63.93% to 74.36% of the total population, can be expected to be negatively impacted by disengagement.

19. Apostoleris (2000), Berg and Corpus (2013), Gray (2013), Gray and Chanoff (1986), Gray and Feldman (2004), Vedder-Weiss and Fortus (2011).

20. Organizations that are at the forefront of the democratic education movement include AERO (Alternative Education Resource Organization) at http://www.educationrevolution.org/, IDEA (Institute for Democratic Education in America) at http://www.democraticeducation.com, and ASDE (Association for Self-Directed Education) at https://www.self-directed.org

21. Siegel (2010)

22. See endnote 9 above.

23. See And 'Rithmetic by Daniel Greenberg URL: http://www.scribd.com/doc/14389275/And-Rithmetic-by-Daniel-Greenberg

24. See Education Laws and Regulations: Policy Statement: School Day and Structured Student Learning Time Requirements: November 2012 URL: http://www.doe.mass.edu/news/news.aspx?id=6682

25. Flanagan (1993), Johnson (1993), Lakoff and Johnson (1999), Lakoff (1996).

26. Flanagan (1993), Johnson (1993).

27. To be clear, wholesale adoption of democratic schooling based on those models would be great, it just seems like an utterly impractical expectation given how hard it is to accomplish large-scale organizational change. Building on the strengths of existing organizational arrangements toward more democratic forms of governance appears to me to be a better approach to change. I believe the gap between the mainstream and the types of alternatives I've highlighted is smaller than it may appear.

28. See endnote 3 above.

29. UNICEF has two school improvement programs: Rights Respecting Schools: https://www.unicef.org.uk/rights-respecting-schools/ & Child Friendly Schools: https://www.unicef.org/lifeskills/index_7260.html

30. See the National Center for Education Statistics Fast Facts on Bullying: https://nces.ed.gov/fastfacts/display.asp?id=719

31. The Hope Survey is one instrument that is scientifically validated for this use. https://www.hopesurvey.org

32. The following citations include research showing the connections between need support, motivation, engagement, and academic and other valued outcomes. Amabile (1996), Assor, Roth, and Deci (2004), Assor, Kaplan, Kanat-Maymon, and Roth (2005), Baard, Deci, and Ryan (2004), Corpus, Mcclintic-Gilbert, and Hayenga (2009), Deci and Ryan (2000, 2012), Dupont, Galand, Nils, and Hospel (2014), Gottfried (1985), Gottfried, Fleming, and Gottfried (2001), Harter (1981), Harter and Jackson (1992), Lepper, Corpus, and Iyengar (2005), Meece, Blumenfeld, and Hoyle (1988), Otis, Grouzet, and Pelletier (2005), Pintrich and Garcia (1991), Ryan and Connell (1989), Ryan and Deci (2000a, 2000b, 2006), Schüler, Brandstätter, and Sheldon (2012), in reference to the need for competence; for summaries of intrinsic motivation research, see Sansone and Harackiewicz (2007) and Stipek (2002).

33. Apostoleris (2000), Berg and Corpus (2013), Gray (2013), Gray and Chanoff (1986), Gray and Feldman (2004), Van Ryzin (2011), Van Ryzin, Gravely, and Roseth (2009), Vedder-Weiss and Fortus (2011).

34. Berg and Allen (2017).

35. Fredricks (2014).

36. One of the ways that we humans have developed to optimize our interactions with our environment is the formation of organizations and societies (organizations of organizations). Organizations are human social structures that restrict the possibilities for human behavior by means of altering how the individual human agents conceptualize their behavioral opportunities and obligations. But they do that within the context of lived experience. The challenge every individual human faces is the same: achieve an ideal match between their conceptual maps of those lived experiences and the reality of the environment such that the result determines behavioral options that match the given obligations and available opportunities in the present situation.

37. I chose the phrase "playfully have fun" to provide a phrasing that would match a child's level of understanding of an everyday experience of optimal states of mind. This draws on the work of Mihaly Csikszentmihalyi on flow as a state of mind that is, by definition, optimal. A couple of the most common methods of accessing flow states are conversation and reading. I suspect that playing is the most common for children. One of the design criteria that I set for myself when I started formulating this map was that it should be useful for directing children as young as four years old. That was the age at which many of the democratic schools I was familiar with began to enroll students. I do not expect the children to understand the whole map, but the part that applies to them should be stated in terms that they can understand.

38. Tyack (1974), Tyack and Cuban (1995), Lortie (2002).

39. Appleton (2000).

40. IMDb listing: http://www.imdb.com/title/tt1042913/
    YouTube Link: https://www.youtube.com/watch?v=TxngqMavda0

41. Dewey (1997).

42. See the Virtues Project: https://www.virtuesproject.com

43. The components are a synthesis of elements drawn from the following books: Mihaly Csikszentmihalyi's *Flow* (1991), Martin Seligman's *Authentic Happiness* (2002), and Kenneth W. Thomas's *Intrinsic Motivation at Work* (2000).

44. Hargreaves and Fullan (2012).

45. Al Jazeera Opinions: http://america.aljazeera.com/opinions/2016/1/why-does-the-media-ignore-high-school-activism.html

46. http://www.npr.org/sections/ed/2015/07/16/420837531/testing-revolt-in-washington-state-brings-feds-into-uncharted-waters

47. An organization has a state of mind in the same way that an organism does since all organizations also have to processes for monitoring and modifying flows of energy and information.

48. Hanson and Yosifon (2004), Zimbardo (2013).

49. Read the book *The Lucifer Effect* (2013) by Stanford psychologist Philip Zimbardo for two extreme real world examples.

# References

AEE (Alliance for Excellent Education). (n.d.). What about deeper learning. Deeper Learning. Retrieved May 18, 2017, from http://deeperlearning4all.org/about-deeper-learning

AIR (American Institutes for Research) & Hewlett Foundation. (n.d.). Study of deeper learning: Opportunities and outcomes. Retrieved May 29, 2017, from http://www.air.org/project/study-deeper-learning-opportunities-and-outcomes

Amabile, T. M. (1996). *Creativity in context: Update to the social psychology of creativity.* Boulder, CO: Westview Press.

Apostoleris, N. (2000). *Children's love of learning: Home schooling and intrinsic motivation for learning* (Doctoral dissertation). Department of Psychology, Clark University, Worcester, Massachusetts. Retrieved from nicholas.apostoleris.net/dissertation.pdf

Appleton, M. (2000). *Free range childhood: Self-regulation at Summerhill School.* Brandon, VT: The Foundation for Educational Renewal, Inc.

Assor, A., Kaplan, H., Kanat-Maymon, Y., & Roth, G. (2005). Directly controlling teacher behaviors as predictors of poor motivation and engagement in girls and boys: The role of anger and anxiety. *Learning and Instruction, 15*(5), 397–413. doi:10.1016/j.learninstruc.2005.07.008

Assor, A., Roth, G., & Deci, E. L. (2004). The emotional costs of parents conditional regard: A self-determination theory analysis. *Journal of Personality, 72*(1), 47–88. doi:10.1111/j.0022-3506.2004.00256.x

Atherton, J. (2013). Approaches to study: "Deep" and "surface." Retrieved April 21, 2017, from http://doceo.co.uk/l&t/learning/deepsurf.htm

Baard, P. P., Deci, E. L., & Ryan, R. M. (2004). Intrinsic need satisfaction: A motivational basis of performance and Weil-Being in two work settings. *Journal of Applied Social Psychology, 34*(10), 2045–2068. doi:10.1111/j.1559-1816.2004.tb02690.x

Bellanca, J. A. (Ed.). (2015). *Deeper learning: Beyond 21st century skills.* Bloomington, IN: Solution Tree Press. ISBN 978-1-936763-35-1

Berg, D., & Allen, H. (2017). *Most schools won't fit: Every parent's dilemma and what to do about it.* West Linn, OR: Attitutor Media.

Berg, D. A., & Corpus, J. H. (2013). Enthusiastic students: A study of motivation in two alternatives to mandatory instruction. *Other Education, 2*(2), 42–66.

Berry, Barnett. (2016). *Teacher leadership & deeper learning for all students*. Rep. Carrboro, NC: Center for Teaching Quality. Print. Retrieved from https://www.teachingquality.org/deeperlearning

Corpus, J. H., Mcclintic-Gilbert, M. S., & Hayenga, A. O. (2009). Within-year changes in children's intrinsic and extrinsic motivational orientations: Contextual predictors and academic outcomes. *Contemporary Educational Psychology, 34*(2), 154–166. doi:10.1016/j.cedpsych.2009.01.001

Csikszentmihalyi, M. (1991). *Flow: The psychology of optimal experience*. New York, NY: Harper Perennial.

Deci, E. L., & Ryan, R. M. (2000). The "what" and "why" of goal pursuits: Human needs and the self-determination of behavior. *Psychological Inquiry, 11*(4), 227–268. doi:10.1207/s15327965pli1104_01

Deci, E. L., & Ryan, R. M. (2012). Motivation, personality, and development within embedded social contexts: An overview of self-determination theory. In Richard M. Ryan (Ed.), *Oxford handbook of human motivation* (pp. 85–107). Oxford: Oxford University Press. doi:10.1093/oxfordhb/9780195399820.001.0001

Dewey, J. (1997). *Experience and education*. New York, NY: Touchstone. Originally published in 1938.

Dewey, J., & Dewey, E. (1962). *Schools of tomorrow: A classic text in the history of American education*. New York, NY: E.P. Dutton & Co., Inc. Originally published in 1915.

Dirkswager, E. J., Farris-Berg, K., & Junge, A. (2012). *Trusting teachers with school success: What happens when teachers call the shots*. Lanham, MD: Rowan & Littlefield Education.

Dunleavy, J., & Milton, P. (2010). Student engagement for effective teaching and deep learning. *Education Canada*, pp. 4–8. Canadian Education Association (cea-ace.ca).

Dupont, S., Galand, B., Nils, F., & Hospel, V. (2014). Social context, self-perceptions and student engagement: A SEM investigation of the self-system model of motivational development (SSMMD). *Electronic Journal of Research in Educational Psychology, 12*(1), 5–32. doi:10.14204/ejrep.32.13081

Entwhistle, N. (2003). *Promoting deep learning through teaching and assessment: Conceptual frameworks and educational contexts*. Proceedings of ESRC Teaching and Learning Research Programme, First Annual Conference, University of Leicester. Retrieved May 11, 2017, from https://www.researchgate.net/publication/241049278_Promoting_

deep_learning_through_teaching_and_assessment_Conceptual_frameworks_and_
educational_contexts

Flanagan, O. (1993). *Varieties of moral personality: Ethics and psychological realism.* Cambridge, MA: Harvard University Press.

Fredricks, J. A. (2014). *Eight myths of disengaged students: Creating classrooms of deep learning.* Thousand Oaks, CA: Corwin Press.

Fullan, M., & Quinn, J. (2016). *Coherence: The right drivers in action for schools, districts, and systems.* Thousand Oaks, CA: Corwin.

Gallup, Inc. (2016). Gallup student poll: Engaged today—Ready for tomorrow: U.S. overall: Fall 2016 scorecard. Publication. Retrieved May 29, 2017, from http://www.gallupstudentpoll.com/197492/2016-national-scorecard.aspx

Gardner, H. (2004). *The unschooled mind: How children think and how schools should teach.* New York: Basic Books.

Gottfried, A. E. (1985). Academic intrinsic motivation in elementary and junior high school students. *Journal of Educational Psychology, 77*(6), 631–645. doi:10.1037//0022-0663.77.6.631

Gottfried, A. E., Fleming, J. S., & Gottfried, A. W. (2001). Continuity of academic intrinsic motivation from childhood through late adolescence: A longitudinal study. *Journal of Educational Psychology, 93*(1), 3–13. doi:10.1037//0022-0663.93.1.3

Gray, P. (2013). *Free to learn: Why unleashing the instinct to play will make our children happier, more self-reliant, and better students for life.* New York, NY: Basic Books.

Gray, P., & Chanoff, D. (1986). Democratic schooling: What happens to young people who have charge of their own education? *American Journal of Education, 94*(2), 182–213. Retrieved from http://www.jstor.org/stable/1084948

Gray, P., & Feldman, J. (2004). Playing in the zone of proximal development: Qualities of self-directed age mixing between adolescents and young children at a democratic school. *American Journal of Education, 110*(2), 108–145. Retrieved from http://www.jstor.org/stable/10.1086/380572

Hanson, J., & Yosifon, D. (2004). The situational character: A critical realist perspective on the human animal. *Georgetown Law Journal, 93*(1), 1–179. Retrieved from http://digitalcommons.law.scu.edu/facpubs/59

Hargreaves, A., & Fullan, M. (2012). *Professional capital: Transforming teaching in every school.* New York, NY: Teachers College Press.

Harter, S. (1981). A new self-report scale of intrinsic versus extrinsic orientation in the classroom: Motivational and informational components. *Developmental Psychology, 17*(3), 300–312. doi:10.1037//0012-1649.17.3.300

Harter, S., & Jackson, B. K. (1992). Trait vs. nontrait conceptualizations of intrinsic/extrinsic motivational orientation. *Motivation and Emotion, 16*(3), 209–230. doi:10.1007/bf00991652

Hastings, M., & Agrawal, S. (2015). Lack of teacher engagement linked to 2.3 million missed workdays. Gallup.com. Retrieved May 18, 2017, from http://www.gallup.com/poll/180455/lack-teacher-engagement-linked-million-missed-workdays.aspx

How Long Does a Female Frog Keep Eggs Inside Her Body? (n.d.). Retrieved August 22, 2017, from http://animals.mom.me/long-female-frog-keep-eggs-inside-her-body-10855.html

IDEA (Institute for Democratic Education in America). (2012). *The vision, strategy, and learning of IDEA (Rep.)* (p. 4). Jackson, MS: IDEA. Retrieved September 20, 2017, from http://democraticeducation.org/downloads/2012_strategy6.pdf

Johnson, M. (1993). *Moral imagination: Implications of cognitive science for ethics.* Chicago, IL: University of Chicago Press.

Kavelin Popov, L., Popov, D., & Kavelin, J. (1997). *The family virtues guide: Simple ways to bring out the best in our children and ourselves.* New York, NY: Penguin Group.

Kim, A. (2015). *Personalized learning playbook: Why the time is now... and how to do it.* Washington, DC: Education Elements.

Kysilko, D. (Ed.). (2014). The State Education Standard, March 2014. Retrieved from http://www.nasbe.org/wp-content/uploads/Standard_Mar2014_full_online.pdf

Lakoff, G. (1996). *Moral politics: What conservatives know that liberals don't.* Chicago, IL: University of Chicago Press.

Lakoff, G., & Johnson, M. (1999). *Philosophy in the flesh: The cognitive unconscious and the embodied mind: How the embodied mind creates philosophy.* New York, NY: Basic Books.

Lepper, M. R., Corpus, J. H., & Iyengar, S. S. (2005). Intrinsic and extrinsic motivational orientations in the classroom: Age differences and academic correlates. *Journal of Educational Psychology, 97*(2), 184–196. doi:10.1037/0022-0663.97.2.184

Lortie, D. C. (2002). *Schoolteacher: With a new preface.* Chicago, IL: University of Chicago Press. Original published 1975.

Marks, H. M. (2000). Student engagement in instructional activity: Patterns in the elementary, middle, and high school years. *American Educational Research Journal, 37*(1), 153–184. doi:10.3102/00028312037001153

Martinez, M. (2014). 6 Rules to break for better, deeper-learning outcomes. Edutopia. Retrieved May 11, 2017, from https://www.edutopia.org/blog/rules-to-break-deeper-learning-monica-martinez

Meece, J. L., Blumenfeld, P. C., & Hoyle, R. H. (1988). Students goal orientations and cognitive engagement in classroom activities. *Journal of Educational Psychology, 80*(4), 514–523. doi:10.1037//0022-0663.80.4.514

Mehta, J., & Fine, S. (2015). *The why, what, where, and how of deeper learning in American secondary schools.* Report. Students at the Center: Deeper Learning Research Series. Boston, MA: Jobs for the Future. Retrieved from http://studentsatthecenterhub.org/resource/the-why-what-where-and-how-of-deeper-learning-in-american-secondary-schools/

Miller, M. R., Latham, B., & Cahill, B. (2017). *Humanizing the education machine: How to create schools that turn disengaged kids into inspired learners.* Hoboken, NJ: John Wiley & Sons.

NASBE (National Association of State Boards of Education, The). (n.d.). About NASBE. Retrieved May 11, 2017, from http://www.nasbe.org/about-us/about-nasbe/

NCES (National Center for Education Statistics). (2016). Fast facts: Dropout rate. National Center for Education Statistics (NCES), a part of the U.S. Department of Education. Retrieved May 18, 2017, from https://nces.ed.gov/fastfacts/display.asp?id=16

Nord, C., Roey, S., Perkins, R., Lyons, M., Lemanski, N., Brown, J., & Schuknecht, J. (2011). *The nation's report card: America's high school graduates* (NCES 2011-462). U.S. Department of Education, National Center for Education Statistics. Washington, DC: U.S. Government Printing Office.

NPDL (New Pedagogies for Deep Learning). (n.d.). Homepage – New pedagogies for deep learning. Retrieved April 30, 2017, from http://npdl.global/

Otis, N., Grouzet, F. M. E., & Pelletier, L. G. (2005). Latent motivational change in an academic setting: A 3-year longitudinal study. *Journal of Educational Psychology, 97*(2), 170–183. doi:10.1037/0022-0663.97.2.170

Pintrich, P. R., & Garcia, T. (1991). Student goal orientation and self-regulation in the college classroom. In M. L. Maehr and P. R. Pintrich (Eds.), *Advances in Motivation and Achievement* (pp. 371-402). Greenwich, CT: JAI Press.

Robinson, K., & Aronica, L. (2016). *Creative schools.* New York, NY: Penguin Books.

Ryan, R. M., & Connell, J. P. (1989). Perceived locus of causality and internalization: Examining reasons for acting in two domains. *Journal of Personality and Social Psychology, 57*(5), 749–761. doi:10.1037//0022-3514.57.5.749

Ryan, R. M., & Deci, E. L. (2000a). Self-determination theory and the facilitation of intrinsic motivation, social development, and well-being. *American Psychologist, 55*(1), 68–78. doi:10.1037//0003-066x.55.1.68

Ryan, R. M., & Deci, E. L. (2000b). The darker and brighter sides of human existence: Basic psychological needs as a unifying concept. *Psychological Inquiry, 11*(4), 319–338. doi:10.1207/s15327965pli1104_03

Ryan, R. M., & Deci, E. L. (2006). Self-regulation and the problem of human autonomy: Does psychology need choice, self-determination, and will? *Journal of Personality, 74*(6), 1557–1586. doi:10.1111/j.1467-6494.2006.00420.x

Sansone, C., & Harackiewicz, J. M. (Eds.). (2007). *Intrinsic and extrinsic motivation: The search for optimal motivation and performance.* San Diego, CA: Academic Press.

Schüler, J., Brandstätter, V., & Sheldon, K. M. (2012). Do implicit motives and basic psychological needs interact to predict well-being and flow? Testing a universal hypothesis and a matching hypothesis. *Motivation and Emotion, 37*(3), 480–495. doi:10.1007/s11031-012-9317-2

Seligman, M. E. (2002). *Authentic happiness: Using the new positive psychology to realize your potential for lasting fulfillment.* New York, NY: Free Press.

Siegel, D. J. (2010). *Mindsight: The new science of personal transformation.* New York, NY: Bantam Books.

Stipek, D. J. (2002). *Motivation to learn: Integrating theory and practice* (4th ed.). Boston, MA: Allyn and Bacon.

Thomas, K. W. (2000). *Intrinsic motivation at work: Building energy & commitment.* San Francisco, CA: Berrett-Koehler.

Trilling, B. (2014). Deeper learning: A new model of transformation. P21.org (web log). Volume 1, Issue 9, Number 14. Retrieved April 30, 2017, from http://www.p21.org/news-events/p21blog/1549-deeper-learning-a-new-model-of-transformation

Tyack, D., & Cuban, L. (1995). *Tinkering toward utopia: A century of public school reform.* Cambridge, MA: Harvard University Press.

Tyack, D. B. (1974). *The one best system: A history of American urban education.* Cambridge, MA: Harvard University Press.

Van Ryzin, M. J. (2011). Protective factors at school: Reciprocal effects among adolescents' perceptions of the school environment, engagement in learning, and hope. *Journal of Youth and Adolescence, 40*(12): 1568–1580. doi:10.1007/s10964-011-9637-7

Van Ryzin, M. J., Gravely, A. A., & Roseth, C. J. (2009). Autonomy, belongingness, and engagement in school as contributors to adolescent psychological well-being. *Journal of Youth and Adolescence, 38*(1), 1–12. doi:10.1007/s10964-007-9257-4

Vedder-Weiss, D., & Fortus, D. (2011). Adolescents' declining motivation to learn science: Inevitable or not? *Journal of Research in Science Teaching, 48*(2), 199–216. doi:10.1002/tea.20398

Washor, E., & Mojkowski, C. (2014). Dialing authenticating connecting: Thinking differently and deeply about student engagement. >, March 2014, 24–31. National Association of State Boards of Education (nasbe.org).

Zhao, Y. (2009). *Catching up, or, Leading the way: American education in the age of globalization.* Alexandria, VA: Association for Supervision and Curriculum Development.

Zimbardo, P. (2013). *The Lucifer effect: Understanding how good people turn evil.* New York, NY: Random House.

# About the Author

Don Berg is an education psychology researcher, alternative education practitioner, leader, and author. The peer-reviewed journals *Other Education* and *The Journal Of The Experimental Analysis Of Behavior* have published his research. He has over 20 years of experience leading children in self-directed educational settings, both in schools and out-of-school programs. In order to help K-12 schools strive for deeper learning he founded Attitutor Services. He serves as an officer on the boards of several educational and political organizations. He co-authored the book *Most Schools Won't Fit* with Holly Allen. The Joyful Llama Ranch in West Linn, Oregon, is his home.

Made in the USA
Columbia, SC
27 November 2017